JN061260

タンポポ

13

TAMPOPO **13**

 ©ユニバーサル ミュージック

すべての食いしん坊に告ぐ。今すぐに『タンポポ』を観よ!

Prologue   A woman's success in operating a ramen shop
is not the point of the film Tampopo.
Through the medium of ramen noodles, director Juzo Itami
wanted to convey a message of "living," "dying," and "eating."
Nearly 40 years after the film's release,
ramen has left its national-dish roots behind
and gone global.
Covid-19, Black Lives Matter,
and Russia's invasion of Ukraine.
The world has been shaken.
Thus, over a bowl of ramen,
we need to reconsider "living," "dying," and "eating."

4   ©伊丹プロダクション

伊丹十三は、ラーメンを隠れ蓑に、「生きること」「死ぬこと」「食べること」の意義をこの映画を通じて伝えたかったのだ。

公開から約40年を経てラーメンは、日本を飛び出して世界の国民食へと昇華した。

新型コロナウィルス、ブラック・ライヴズ・マター、さらにはロシアによるウクライナ侵攻。

世界が揺らぐ今だからこそ、ラーメンをすすりながら改めて、「生きること」「死ぬこと」そして、「食べること」について考える。

To all foodies:
see *Tampopo* right away!

目次

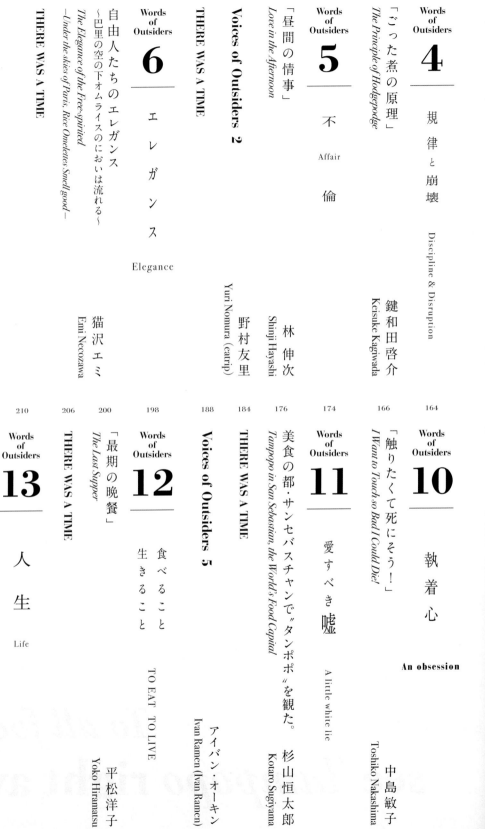

CONTENTS

マナーについて　　　　　The manners

Photograph_Yosuke Suzuki　　　Styling_Miwako Tanaka

Words of Outsiders

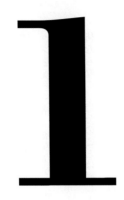

「映画はじまってからその音立てたら、俺、アンタのこと**殺す**かもしれないからね」

Make that noise after the film starts

and I might **kill you.**

『タンポポ』の悦楽的ニヒリズム

菅付雅信

#メタ映画としての『タンポポ』

この映画は映画館のシーンから始まる。これは「映画についての映画」であることをのっけから宣言するかのように。

冒頭、役所広司演じるヤクザが情婦と手下を従え、映画館に入ってくる。ヤクザは手下が用意したシャンパンを女と一緒に嗜みながら映画を楽しもうとするが、後ろの席の男性がかじるポテトチップスの音が我慢ならない。自分のことは棚に上げ、その男性の映画館におけるマナーの悪さを叱責して悦に入ったところで、唐突に本編が始まる。そう、これは「マナーについての」のシニカルな表現でもある。『タンポポ』は映画を、そして映画を観る作法を斜め上の視点から捉えた態度表明で幕を開ける。

『タンポポ』公開時のキャッチ・コピーは「ラーメン・ウェスタン」というものだ。物語の構造としては、寂れた街の、しかも乱暴者に脅されているラーメン屋の女主人＝タンポポを、風来坊／はぐれものの男＝ゴローが助けて、問題を解決し、去っていく内容だ。つまり、西部劇の典型的物語構造に則っている。

さらに『タンポポ』は黒澤映画へのオマージュでもある。

黒澤明が最も影響を受けた映画監督は西部劇の

ジョン・フォード。よって黒澤は時代劇を西部劇のように撮ろうと試みた。その結果が『用心棒』『隠し砦の三悪人』『七人の侍』に結実している。よって伊丹十三も、物語構造は西部劇だが、本編の随所随所で黒澤へのオマージュを企てている。文字の書体や移動ショット、人物ショットのあちこちに黒澤へのオマージュがある。

よって、『タンポポ』はラーメンならびに食を題材にした西部劇構造の物語を黒澤のように撮るという、二重の「本歌取り」をしている。いわば西部劇と黒澤映画のメタ映画でもある。

#非・映画としての『タンポポ』

さらに、『タンポポ』の独創的な部分は、映画のあちこちに出てくる、本編とは関係ない食に関するうんちくやエピソード。特に役所広司が演じるグルメなヤクザのパートは本編と何の関係もない。しかし、この役所ヤクザの断続的なエピソードが、セックスや暴力、死といった映画の根源的な題材を鮮烈に表し、本編を超えるくらいのインパクトがある。

つまり、『タンポポ』の本編＝西部劇的な、ある種の紋切り型の物語にわざと邪魔をするかのような、本

Tampopo: The Joy of Nihilism

Masanobu Sugatsuke

Tampopo as a meta-movie

Tampopo begins with a scene in a movie theater as if declaring from the very beginning that it is a movie about movies.

At the start, the yakuza gangster played by Koji Yakushi, accompanied by his moll and his underlings, comes into the theater. Sipping with the woman the champagne his men have brought for him, he prepares to enjoy the film but is unable to abide the sound of a man crunching potato chips in a seat behind him. Blind to his own behavior, he is increasingly enjoying himself, scolding the man for his poor theater manners when suddenly the "real movie" begins. Yes, this is a cynical representation of the manners involved in talking about other people's manners. The curtain rises on *Tampopo* both as a film and as an unexpected attitude statement on how films should be viewed.

At the time of its release, *Tampopo* was billed as a "ramen western." In the story, a lone drifter, Goro, comes to the rescue of Tampopo, the woman proprietor trying to run a ramen restaurant in a lonely part of town while being threatened by a group of hoodlums. Goro, having solved her problems, goes on his way. In short,

this follows the classic structure of a western.

Tampopo is also an homage to Kurosawa films. The director who most heavily influenced Akira Kurosawa was the western-movie director John Ford. As a result, Kurosawa tried to make Japanese period films in the manner of western movies. *Yojimbo, The Hidden Fortress,* and *Seven Samurai* are the result. Thus Juzo Itami also structures his story as a western, but the film itself is designed as an homage to Kurosawa. The style of the lettering, the tracking shots, the people shots; the homage to Kurosawa is everywhere.

Tampopo is thus a two-layered adaptation of a story about ramen and foods shot in a classic western structure in Kurosawa style. In other words, it is a "meta-movie" of both western films and Kurosawa.

Tampopo as an "un-movie"

Another unique element of *Tampopo* is the variety of food-related lore and assorted episodes scattered throughout the film that bears no relation to its central plot. In particular, the scenes featuring Koji Yakusho as the gangster gourmet have no connection with the main story.

編と関係がない、しかし食とは関係があるエピソードがあちこちに織り込まれているというのは、伝統的な映画にはない構造。しかし、伊丹十三という人のマルチ・クリエイター性は――それを雑食性と言ってもいい――映画を伝統的なストラクチャーから変容させようと試みた。よって、伊丹がエッセイストであり、雑誌編集長（『モノンクル』）であり、テレビ番組制作者であり、テレビCMの演出家でもあるマルチな多様性――それを80年代に流行した現代思想の言葉を用いると「分裂症的／スキゾフレニック」（©浅田彰）とも呼べるが――を活かして、本来はリニアな物語展開がある映画という伝統的なアート・フォームのリコンストラクションを試みている。

よって、この『タンポポ』は、ラーメンを軸としながらも、食全般を題材としたスキゾフレニックな映画となっており、それは雑誌的とも言えるし、テレビ番組的とも言える。よって「こんなの映画じゃないよ」という当時の批判は、伊丹が意図して狙ったところではないかと思える。ただし、そういう批判は彼の予想を超えた辛辣さがあったはずだ。

『タンポポ』は伊丹十三究極の作家映画

『タンポポ』を伊丹のフィルモグラフィーの中で捉え直すと、これは伊丹の監督二作目。一作目の『お葬式』が大変高い評価を受け、興行的にも成功した後の期待の第二作だったが、一部の評論家からは評価を得たものの、興行的には失敗する。そして一作目と二作目は共に山崎努が主演を務め、宮本信子がサブになるが、三作目の『マルサの女』から、主に宮本信子を主演した女性が活躍し、ストレートにリニアな物語進行と、明確なカタルシスがあるエンタメ映画になる。

また『タンポポ』は、役所広司のヤクザのパートが重要な位置を占め、このグルメでキザなヤクザのセリフが極めて伊丹十三的。よって山崎努と役所広司のふたりの好対照なキャラクターの両方に、伊丹十三はかなり自身を投影させていると言っていいだろう。

そして、前述のメタ映画構造、スキゾフレニックな非・映画構造という、「遅れてきた映画監督」としてやりたい手法を存分に投入した仕上がりは、当時の一般的な観客からの反応は悪かったが、時間が経つにつれ、内外共に評価が高まり、今では伊丹映画の中で最も評価の高い一本になっている。

However, these unconnected yakuza episodes vividly make clear the film's fundamental themes of sex, violence, and death and have an impact that may even exceed that central story.

This structure, where episodes that have nothing to do with the story outside of their connection with food interrupt the stereotypical western-like main plot, is not that of a traditional motion picture. However, in his wide-ranging—one might even say "omnivorous"—creativity, Juzo Itami is trying to transform the traditional film structure. Putting to use his wide-ranging creativity as an essayist, a magazine editor (*monocle*), a television producer, and a TV commercial director—"schizophrenic," to use a word popular in the 1980s to describe a modern concept (coined by Akira Asada)—he tries to reconstruct the classic linear story development of the traditional art form known as a "movie."

Therefore *Tampopo*, while it centers on ramen, is a schizophrenic film whose theme is food in general, shot in a magazine-like and a TV program-like manner. Thus it seems Itami was deliberately aiming for the criticism leveled at the time that it was "not a movie." That criticism, however, was probably harsher than he had expected.

Tampopo as Juzo Itami's Ultimate Auteur's Film

Looking back at Juzo Itami's filmography, *Tampopo* was his second motion picture. Expectations were high following the critical and box-office success of his first film, *The Funeral*, and while *Tampopo* was highly rated by some critics, it was a commercial failure. While his first and second films feature Tsutomu Yamazaki in the leading role with Nobuko Miyamoto in a secondary role, his third film, *A Taxing Woman*, features Miyamoto as the star, and his stories develop in a straight linear fashion, as entertainment with a clear catharsis.

Again, in *Tampopo*, Koji Yakusho's yakuza part occupies an important place, and the lines spoken by this pretentious gourmet gangster are very much characteristic of Juzo Itami. Thus it can probably be said that Itami is projecting himself into the two contrasting characters of Tsutomu Yamazaki and Koji Yakusho.

General audiences at the time did not respond well to this late-blooming director's use of any technique he felt moved to incorporate in this "meta/schizophrenic un-movie." But with time, its reputation has risen in Japan and abroad, and

私が編集したNY出身のアイバン・オーキンが東京で開いたラーメン屋に関する本『アイバンのラーメン』(リトルモア／2008年)でも、オーキンがラーメンに興味を持ったのは米国で見た『タンポポ』に衝撃を受けたからだと語っている。

「映画自体は、僕にとって単なるラーメンの映画ではなかった。この映画でラーメンは、あくまで話を運ぶためのヴィークル(乗り物)。ラーメン屋を題材に、レストランでいかにお客さんにハッピーになってもらうかを描いていると思ったんだ。(略)すっかり『タンポポ』を気に入って、何度も繰り返し劇場で見た。(略)もしこの映画と出会わなかったら、間違いなく今の僕はラーメン屋を始めていない」(『アイバンのラーメン』より)

このほかにも内外で様々な受け止められ方をされた『タンポポ』は、伊丹映画のフィルモグラフィーの中では異例の作品として見做されながらも、実はこれこそが伊丹の究極の作家映画だと断言したい。彼のエッセンス(それは美点だけに限らない)が一番濃密に含まれているのが『タンポポ』なのだ。

自分が一番うんちくを語れる食をテーマに、大好きな西部劇と黒澤映画をオマージュし、愛する妻の宮本信子を助ける誠実さと、不倫問題で騒がれたことがある不実さとをないまぜにして、役所ヤクザのように美味しいものを想像しながらスクリーンの中で果てるという夢を叶えた、伊丹シェフおまかせのフルコース映画。伊丹がやりたいように作った分裂症的ガストロノミーとも言える。

『タンポポ』の一部の批評的成功と興行的な失敗が、その後の伊丹をエンタメの映画づくりに専念することを強いることになる。そういう点でも『タンポポ』は伊丹十三にとって、最も重要なベンチマークになる作品と言えるだろう。伊丹は『タンポポ』というヴィークル=乗り物に、やりたいことを思い切り詰め込んで吐き出すことで、自分の映画監督としての可能性と限界を認識したはずだ。自分は活劇作家としては黒澤にもジョン・フォードにもセルジオ・レオーネにもなれなく、また芸術的映画作家(オーサー)として敬愛するルイス・ブニュエルのように美学を極めることもできないと。しかし、活劇も芸術もないまぜにした新しい分裂症的な映画は作れるぞと。この映画の中でラーメンと舌平目のムニエルを同列に扱うように。

それが伊丹の屈折した、しかしひとつ上のレイヤーの視点を獲得した新たなダンディズムでもある。『タ

it is now the most highly rated Juzo Itami film.

In a book I edited, *Ivan's Ramen* (Little Moa 2008), the New York native Ivan Orkin writes that seeing *Tampopo* in the U.S. inspired him to move to Tokyo and open a ramen restaurant.

"For me, the film itself was not just a ramen movie. In it, ramen is simply a vehicle to carry the story. The ramen shop, I thought, was a theme for a movie about a restaurant making people happy...I loved *Tampopo*, and at the theater, I saw it again and again...if I hadn't encountered that movie, I am sure the person I am now would never have started a ramen restaurant. " (from *Ivan's Ramen*)

Besides this, *Tampopo* has been received in various ways both inside Japan and abroad. And though it might be considered an outlier in the Itami filmography, I want to assert that it is Itami's ultimate auteur's film. It is *Tampopo* that (for better or worse) most richly distills his essence.

This film is Chef Itami's full-course chef's choice movie, a film whose theme is food—a subject on which he can speak with great erudition—and a film that is also both an homage to western and to Kurosawa movies and an act of support for his beloved wife Nobuko Miyamoto even among rumors of infidelity. There are parallels between how Itami achieves his dream with Yakusho's on-screen gangster, who is shot to death imagining the ultimate delicious food.

The partial critical success and box-office failure of *Tampopo* would later force Itami to focus on making entertainment films. In this respect, *Tampopo* is the most important benchmark work for Juzo Itami. By cramming together and pouring out everything he wanted to do through this vehicle of *Tampopo*, Itami must have recognized both his possibilities and limitations as a film director. He was not an action director like Kurosawa, John Ford, or Sergio Leone, nor was he an artistic "author" who could take esthetics to an extreme like Luis Buñuel, for whom he had deep respect. He could, however, make a new schizophrenic film that combined both action and art in the way the movie gives the same treatment to both ramen and sole meunière.

Tampopo is Itami's new dandyism that is refracted but has acquired the perspective of one layer above. *Tampopo* is also a "chimera" of a movie that emerged in the flow of the post-

ンポポ」は「ポストモダン」という言葉が流行し、その言葉が意味する、大きな物語や理念を喪失した後に、小さな物語やイメージを折衷的に束ねて新たな表現／考え方として提示することを肯定する、80年代以降の日本の文化潮流のなかで生まれたキメラ（異質同体）のような映画でもある。

しかし、このようなポストモダン的な振る舞いは、ある種のニヒリズムにも陥りやすい。もはやドラマティックな物語も芸術至上主義も存在しえないのだと。様々なメディアでやや露悪的に開示していた伊丹のスタイリッシュな振る舞いと言動ならびに表現活動は、当時の日本社会に対してニヒリスト的な立ち位置に見えていたはずだ。

実は私は編集者として伊丹にインタビューの現場でお会いしているのだが（『CUT』1990年7月号／NO.4）、インタビュアーを務めた渋谷陽一の質問に常に反論するかのように答える伊丹の偏屈な姿勢に困惑した経験がある。伊丹は――彼自身のエッセイに特徴的だが――常にいろんなものに怒り、嘆いていた。一方では食や旅行、そして映画づくりには並々ならぬ快楽を感じていた。そう、役所広司演じるグルメなヤクザのように、伊丹は悦楽的ニヒリストなのだ。そしてそのことに彼は自覚的だ。伊丹は自著であり名著の誉れ高い『女たちよ！』の冒頭でこう書いている。

「私は役に立つことをいろいろと知っている。そうしてその役に立つことを普及もしている。がしかし、これらはすべて人から教わったことばかりだ。私自身は――ほとんどまったく無内容な、空っぽの容れ物にすぎない。」

菅付雅信（すがつけ・まさのぶ）
編集者／株式会社グーテンベルクオーケストラ代表取締役

『コンポジット』『インビテーション』『エココロ』の編集長を務めたのち、現在は編集・執筆から企画、コンサルティングを手がける。著書に『はじめての編集』『物欲なき世界』『写真が終わる前に』等。またアートブック出版社ユナイテッドヴァガボンズの代表も務め、編集・出版した片山真理写真集『GIFT』は木村伊兵衛写真賞を受賞。下北沢B&Bで「編集スパルタ塾」、渋谷パルコで「東京芸術中学」を主宰。東北芸術工科大学教授。NYADC賞銀賞、D&AD賞受賞。

80s Japanese culture, affirming that, after the word "post-modern" has come into play, and after the phrase lost the big stories and ideas it signifies, small-scale stories and images blend to show themselves in new expressions and ways of thinking.

This kind of post-modern behavior, however, can easily fall into a kind of nihilism: the claim that dramatic narratives and "art for art's sake" can no longer exist. Itami's stylish behavior, words, and expressive activities, which the media presented as vaguely louche, must have made him seem like a nihilist to Japanese society at that time.

As it happens, as an editor, I met Itami at a magazine interview (*Cut* No. 4, July 1990.) I was bewildered by his perverse responses, as if he were arguing with the questions posed by Yoichi Shibuya, who served as the interviewer. He seemed—as was characteristic of his essays— to be angrily lamenting any number of things. On the other hand, he found extraordinary pleasure in food, travel, and filmmaking. Yes, just like the gourmet gangster played by Koji Yakusho, Itami was a hedonistic nihilist. And he was aware of this. At the beginning of his well-respected literary work *Listen, Women!* he writes

"I know a lot of useful things. And I am also trying to spread those useful things around. However, these are all things other people have taught me. I myself am no more than an empty vessel containing almost nothing."

Translation_Ian MacDougall

Masanobu Sugatsuke
Editor / President, Gutenberg Orchestra Co., Ltd.

Having served as chief editor for *Composite*, *Invitation*, and *Ecocolo*, Sugatsuke now works at everything from editing and writing to planning and consulting. His published works include *The Way of Edit*, *A World without Desire*, and *Before Photography Is Over*. As president and editor of the art publisher United Vagabonds, Sugatsuke edited and published *Gift*, a collection of photographs by Mari Katayama that won the Kimura Ihei Award for new photographers. Sugatsuke also serves as chairman of "Editing Sparta Seminar" at B&B Books in Tokyo's Shimokitazawa and the "Tokyo Art Junior High" at the Parco department store in Shibuya. He is a professor at the Tohoku University of Art & Design, and has won both an NYADC Silver Cube award and a D&AD Pencil award.

THERE WAS A TIME

Photographs by Parker Fitzgerald

高浜橋（芝浦）

Takahama Bashi, SHIBAURA

Excellent
Supporting
Cast

名
脇
役

Photograph_Shoichi Kajino

Words of Outsiders

I want you quietly to apologize to the pork.

"Until we meet again."

「そしてこれが大切なところですが、

この時心の中で詫びるが如く呟いてほしいのです」

「あとでね と」

わが松山、わがラーメンの焼豚

梶野彰一

松山に育った僕が伊丹十三というおじさんを知ったのは比較的幼い時期であった。そのおじさんは洒脱な原稿を書くエッセイストとしてでもなく、ましてや社会問題に切り込む映画監督としてでもなかった。ただ一六タルトという地方銘菓のテレビのコマーシャルでデフォルメされた伊予弁を話すおじさんとしてその名前を知ったのだ。ちなみに松山でタルトと聞いて、いちごやブルーベリーが乗ったハイカラなタルトを思い浮かべる者はまずいない。子どもの頃から、タルトといえばあんこが「の」の字に巻かれたロールケーキのような体裁のこの甘い菓子のことであった。

そのおじさんが監督したというのが話題になってか、映画『タンポポ』を僕が観たのは、中学生の頃だったように思う。当時の15歳にとってはいくつかの刺激的な映像があって、大人になって見返すまで『タンポポ』は、「生卵が行ったり来たりする映画」として記憶に残っていたくらいだ。全編を通じる〝ラーメン・ウエスタン〟の話こそ記憶の傍に置いてきぼりにさせるほどに『タンポポ』は、食にまつわるエッセイ集のような印象だった。

いくつかあるサイドストーリーのなかでも「ラーメンの作法」を説く冒頭のエピソードは、まさに伊丹節

My Matsuyama, My Roast Pig in Ramen

Shoichi Kajino

Growing up in Matsuyama, I became aware of an old guy named Juzo Itami at a relatively young age. I did not know him as the sophisticated essayist, even less as the director of keenly insightful and socially conscious motion pictures. I knew his name as the man speaking an exaggerated version of the Ehime Prefecture dialect in a commercial for Ichiroku Tart, a local cake manufacturer. Almost no one in Matsuyama thinks of high-class blueberry and strawberry-topped pastries when the word "tart" is mentioned. Instead, from childhood, the word summons a jelly roll cake with a sweet bean-paste filling in the shape of the Japanese Hiragana letter "no," written as の .

Perhaps because people were talking about him as a movie director, I saw the film *Tampopo* when I was in middle school. For a 15-year-old, there were many stimulating movies around, and until I saw *Tampopo* again as an adult, I only vaguely remembered it as the film in which two people passed a raw egg back and forth. My impression was of a collection of essays on food, to the extent that the "ramen western" theme that pervades the movie was left stranded in some back corner of my memory.

あふれたこの映画のイントロダクションであって、こ
こに登場する老人はまるで茶の湯の先生のように目の
前のラーメンへと向かう姿勢を正してくれる。あたか
もカウンターを介して店主と客との間で行われる茶席
のようにラーメン店での行為が描かれ、思わずカウン
ター越しに受け取った器を一度、二度と回してしまい
たくなる。これからカウンターの中に立つ店主のお点
前を鍛錬していくメインストーリーを前に、客人たち
の姿勢を正そうという構えだ。食べる前に愛情を持っ
て箸でラーメンを撫でる行為を凛と指南する老人、特
筆すべきは焼豚（やきぶた）の扱いだろう。

「箸の先で焼豚（やきぶた）を愛おしむようにつつき、
おもむろにつまみあげ、どんぶり右上方の位置に沈ま
せ加減に安置するのです。そしてこれが大切なところ
ですが、この時、心の中で詫びるがごとくつぶやいて
ほしいのです『あとでね』と」。そして麺をすする時も、
視線は右上方の焼豚に注げという。ここで控えめな位
置に置かれた3枚の焼豚は、具材の中では間違いなく
主役だが、ラーメンとスープの存在の前には一気に脇
役に押しやられるのである。

「チャーシュー」ではなく「やきぶた」と呼ぶのに

もそこはかとない懐かしさを感じないではいられない
が、2023年のわれわれが、この焼豚と支那竹とナ
ルトの浮いたあまりにも素っ気のないそのラーメンの
姿を目にすると、この40年の日本のラーメンの進化に
ついて振り返らないではいられなくなってしまう。た
とえば、当時、自分のような中学生は白濁した豚骨ラー
メンの存在を知って驚いたほどの時代だった。ご当地
ラーメンは決してその地から出ることなく、もちろん
「〜系」というジャンルはその片鱗もなかった時代だ。
それが、ラーメンはもはや「中華そば」という呼び名
とともにその出自を忘れ去り、さまざまな融合・進化
を果たし、今や最もポップ＆イージーなジャパニーズ・
フードの一品として世界へと華麗な進出を果たしたの
である。

当然、日本人のお作法も、昭和のそれからは随分と
かけ離れた。今では行列のできるような人気のラーメ
ン店では、多くの客が箸を手にとる前に、スマート
フォンでその湯気たつラーメンの姿を撮影しているの
を目にするだろう。自分のための食事記録なのかソー
シャルメディアにシェアされるものなのかはさてお
き、もはやその行為は一つのお作法のようなものである。電
子シャッター音の後に、箸を手に取り「いただきます」
と麺に一礼をするのである。

But amidst its many side stories, the film's true Itami-like introduction is the opening "etiquette of ramen" episode, with an elderly man explaining the correct way to approach the bowl of ramen in front of one in exactly the style of a tea-ceremony instructor. It is as if the customer and ramen shop owner were a tea-ceremony guest and host separated by a counter, to the degree that you instinctively want to turn the bowl once or twice in the manner of a tea ceremony cup upon receiving it. This segment establishes the correct customer attitude before the beginning of the main story, which involves the cook's training in proper procedure. The elderly man instructs how to elegantly hold one's chopsticks and stroke the ramen noodles before eating. Of particular note is the treatment of the pork slices.

"With the tips of the chopsticks, caress the roast pig slices, then gently take hold of them and situate them in the upper right of the bowl. Then—and this is important—I want you quietly to apologize to the pork. 'Until we meet again.'" Then, when you slurp up the noodles, keep your eyes on the roast pork in the upper right of the bowl. These three pieces of meat, placed thus in an unassuming position, are undoubtedly the featured player among all the ingredients, but compared to the ramen and the soup, they are pushed all at once into a supporting role.

Hearing the meat called the native-Japanese *yakibuta*, or "roast pig," rather than the more sophisticated Chinese-derived *chashu* "roast pork," I can't help but feel faintly nostalgic. Still, in 2023, when I see that simple ramen with just pork, bamboo shoot, and fish cake floating on top, I can't help looking back at the evolution of Japanese ramen from 40 years ago. For example, that was a time when a middle-school student like myself would be astonished to learn of the existence of cloudy white "pork-bone" ramen. In those days, the local version of ramen never left its home area, so of course, not even a glimmer of the so-called "X-style ramen" genre existed. Now, however, along with the memory of it once being called "Chinese-style soba," ramen has forgotten its origins. With various fusions and evolutions, it is making a grand entrance onto the world stage as one of the most "pop" and easily accessed Japanese foods.

Naturally, the manners of the Japanese people have also changed considerably from those of the Showa period in the 1970s and 80s. Now, at

老人が指南した第一段階の箸で麺の表面を撫でて愛でる行為は、現代ではまんべんなく視線を送りカメラをむけるこの撮影行為へと完全に移行しているようだ。

ラーメン文化が萌芽を迎える前夜のような当時の感覚では、庶民の食「ラーメンごとき」にその作法を説くというのは笑止千万であったはずだった。それが今やそのシャッター音を聞くまでもなく、多くの客が一杯のラーメンに愛をもってそれぞれの作法で対峙しているように思えてくるのだ。そして、もはや「ラーメンごとき」という存在ではなくなったようなのは、『タンポポ』を軽々と越えるような、店主の命をかけた一杯の気迫のおかげもあるのだろう。

にしても、翻ってこのエピソードに登場するラーメンの姿の潔さよ。今こそ、こんな「ごとき」ラーメンを僕は食べたくて仕方がなくなってしまう。まさに昭和の松山に育った当時、それ一択しかなく食べていたような一杯を。

個人的な松山の話に戻るが、映画『タンポポ』を観たその頃に高校に進学した僕が、自分の通う母校に「タルトのおじさん」が学んでいたことを知ったのは、しばらく経ってからのことだった。おじさんが卒業したのはどうやらおとなりの高校だったようだが、そもそ

も京都生まれの伊丹さんがどういう経緯で松山に学んだのかなど、その詳細はよく知らないままだった。

在学時、伊丹十三、大江健三郎といった偉大な先達の背中がぼんやり見えるようになったその時期、僕はすでにヨーロッパへの、パリへの憧憬で頭がいっぱいだった。せめてその時期に『ヨーロッパ退屈日記』だけでも読む機会を得なかった、そしてタルトのおじさんの本当の姿に気付かないで過ごしていた自分に、今でも激しい後悔を覚えている。

松山へ帰るたび、僕が一六タルトをいただくようになったのは、ほんの数年前からだ。

梶野彰一（かじの・しょういち）
フォトグラファー／文筆家

伊丹さんの通った松山東高校卒業。その後、パリに魅せられ、フレンチ・カルチャーに溺れる。パリと東京を行ったり来たりしながら写真を撮ったり、文章を書いたりしています。

ramen restaurants popular enough that there are lines to get into them, you see many people with cell phones taking pictures of steaming bowls of ramen before they take chopsticks in hand. Leaving aside whether this is for their personal recollection or to post on social media, this action seems to have become a form of etiquette. After clicking the shutter, they pick up their chopsticks and bow to the noodles with the ritual expression, "I humbly accept this meal."

The elderly man's first step of gently stroking the noodles' surface with his chopsticks seems to have now changed to that of people looking through their cameras in the act of photography.

At that time, with ramen culture only in its beginning stages, it was absurd to lecture on the etiquette of eating that "plain old" ramen, a simple commoner's food. Today, though, no sooner does one hear the sound of restaurant shutters opening then crowds of customers square off against each other over how their particular favorite bowl of ramen should be made. And the disappearance of "plain old" ramen may partly be due to the all-in spirit of ramen shop proprietors, which easily exceeds that of *Tampopo*.

Even so, let us praise the ramen that appears in this episode. Even now, I cannot help but feel an overpowering urge to eat that "plain old" ramen, especially the ramen that was the only choice available when I was growing up in Matsuyama in the 70s and 80s.

Returning to my own tales of Matsuyama, around the time I saw the movie *Tampopo* I had moved on to high school, and it was not until some time later that I learned that the "old Tart guy" had studied at my school. He had, for some reason, graduated from the high school next to ours, but I did not know in detail the circumstances under which the Kyoto-born Mr. Itami had ended up studying in Matsuyama.

While studying there, when it was as if I could faintly see the departing backs of my school's famous alumni, Juzo Itami and Kenzaburo Oe, my head was filled with yearning for Europe and Paris. I still bitterly regret not having the chance to read even Itami's *Diary of Boredom in Europe* at that time and not realizing who the "old Tart guy" really was.

It was only a few years ago that I started to treat myself to an Ichiroku Tart whenever I went back to Matsuyama.

Translation_Ian MacDougall

Shoichi Kajino
Photographer / Writer

Kajino is a graduate of Matsuyama Higashi High School, also attended by Juzo Itami. Falling under the spell of Paris, he immersed himself in French culture. Now as a photographer/writer, he splits his time between Paris and Tokyo.

大井北埠頭橋（品川）
Oi Kita Futo Kyo, SHINAGAWA

ゴロー（山崎努）による指導の下、ランニングに励むタンポポ（宮本信子）が小休憩する。その横をビジネスランチに向かうサラリーマン一行が通り過ぎる。メインストーリーとサイドストーリーが交錯する貴重な場面。

Under the coaching of Goro (Tsutomu Yamazaki), Tampopo (Nobuko Miyamoto) takes a break. The camera leaves them to follow a passing group of businessmen on their way to lunch. An important transition point from main story to side story.

Interview_Makoto Miura (COLAXO)
Photographs_Aya Brackett
Translation_Hiroko Kato (Interview), Trivector Co., Ltd. (Article)

サム・ホワイト（左）＆ レイニエル・デ・グズマン（右）   Sam White (left) & Rayneil De Guzman (right)

Sam White & Rayneil De Guzman

サム・ホワイト & レイニエル・デ・グズマン

【RAMEN SHOP】

映画『タンポポ』を考察する本を作ろうと考え、真っ先に思いつい
た取材先がサンフランシスコはオークランドに店を構える「ラーメ
ンショップ」だった。カリフォルニア・キュイジーヌの母として知
られるアリス・ウォータースが1970年代より営むシェ・パニース。
その卒業生がなぜか開いたラーメン屋で『タンポポ』のポスターを
目にしたのが2017年のことだった。

幼い頃、テレビで何度も再放送を観ていたあの奇妙な映画がアメリ
カでもその存在を知られていることにまず驚いた。帰国後、大人に
なってからはじめて観直した『タンポポ』に、さらに驚かされた。
これが言語の壁を超えて、そしてラーメンのどんぶりから溢れる勢
いで生きること、食べること、はたまたその先の死までも描いてい
る作品であることを遅ればせながら知ったのだから。

ラーメン、アメリカ、タンポポ、シェ・パニース。異物感たっぷり
のバラバラな要素がDJのマッシュアップさながらにまとまってい
くことができたのは、伊丹十三という眩い才能が、常に"人間"と
いう最も難解にして、最も魅力的なテーマを創作の大きな骨組みに
していたからに違いない。

When I thought about making a book on the movie *Tampopo*, the
first interview candidate that came to my mind was Ramen Shop. This
establishment in Oakland, California, had been opened, somewhat
mysteriously to me, by alumni of Chez Panisse – the longstanding restaurant
of Alice Waters, the mother of California Cuisine. It was in 2017 that I saw a
poster there of *Tampopo*.

I was first surprised that this strange film I had seen reruns of many times on
TV as a child was known in the United States. After returning to Japan,
I watched it again for the first time as an adult and was even more surprised –
I belatedly learned that it transcends language barriers to depict living, eating,
and even death with the momentum of ramen overflowing from its bowl.

Ramen, the United States, *Tampopo*, and Chez Panisse. The reason these
disparate elements, which are so foreign to each other, were able to come
together like a DJ mash-up was no doubt that the dizzying talent of Juzo Itami
always took the most challenging and fascinating topic of all –human beings–
as the framework for his creations.

日本人がラーメンのどんぶりを前に 集中 するその所作は、
まるで 儀式 のようで 感動 した。

—「ラーメンショップ」をはじめる前のキャリアについて教えてください

レイ（以下R）：ここにいるサムとシェ・パニースで働いていたんだ。創業メンバーには
同じくシェ・パニースの同僚だった JJ（Jerry Jaksich）もいたけれど、彼は現在日本を
拠点にしている。シェ・パニースは "Farm to Table" をコンセプトに生産者と直接関係
を構築するレストランで、日本でもその存在は知られていると思う。本当に素晴らしい職
場で、素晴らしいシェフたちがいた。生産者との交流やファーマーズ・マーケットでの体
験など、シェ・パニースでの経験がいま「ラーメンショップ」で実践しているすべてのこ
とに繋がっているよ。

サム（以下S）：僕は大学がニューヨークで、19歳のときにイースト・ヴィレッジのバー
で働いていた。卒業してからはニュージーランドに渡って5ヶ月ほど農場で働いて、これ
が食と農業の世界に興味を持つきっかけになった。それからカリフォルニアに戻って働い
たのがシェ・パニース。8年いたよ。つまり僕はオフィスで働いた経験が全然ないんだ（笑）。

— どのようにラーメンを好きになりましたか？

R：子供の頃、学校でお弁当といえばみんなサンドイッチだったけれど、うちの家族にとっ
て食事は温かいことが当たり前だったから、サーモスを持っていってインスタントのラー
メンを食べていたんだ。そんな原体験に加えて、10年以上前に日本を訪れたことが決定
的なきっかけになった。シェ・パニースの常連で日本に移り住んだ日本料理研究家である
ナンシー・ハチスが誘ってくれた旅で、ラーメンはもちろん、寿司やそのほかの日本食に
とても感動したんだ。サムもJJも日本で同じ感動を覚えた。とりわけラーメンにおける
出汁や旨味の追求は、イタリアンフレンチをベースとするシェ・パニースではできないこ
とだったから。

S：それに日本人がラーメンのどんぶりを前に集中するその所作は、まるで儀式のようで感
動した。主食である麺もおかずとなる具材も一緒くたになる様式はアメリカにないものだっ
たし、なにより味にハマった。それに地域ごとにさまざまなスタイルがあって、背景にそ
の土地の文化や歴史があることも魅力的だった。そもそも日本料理における美味しさの構
成要素は西洋料理と異なる。異なるパレットに異なるバランス。これが斬新に感じたんだ。

The way the Japanese concentrated
on the ramen bowl in front of them, like a ritual, was very moving.

Please tell me about your career before starting Ramen Shop.

Ray (R): I used to work at Chez Panisse with Sam here. One of the founding members was JJ (Jerry Jaksich), also my colleague at Chez Panisse, but he is now based in Japan. Chez Panisse is a restaurant that builds direct relationships with producers based on the concept of "Farm to Table." I think it's known in Japan. It was a really great place to work, with great chefs. My experiences at Chez Panisse, such as farmers' markets and interacting with producers, are connected to everything I do now at Ramen Shop.

Sam (S): I went to college in New York City and worked in a bar in the East Village when I was 19. After graduation, I went to New Zealand and worked on a farm for about five months, which sparked my interest in food and agriculture. Then I went back to California and worked at Chez Panisse. I was there for eight years. In other words, I have absolutely no experience working in an office (laugh).

How did you fall in love with ramen?

R: When I was a kid, everyone had sandwiches for lunch at school, but for my family, hot meals were the norm, so I would take a Thermos and eat instant ramen. In addition to that kind of formative experience, visiting Japan more than ten years ago was decisive for me. Nancy Hachisu, a regular at Chez Panisse and a Japanese cuisine expert who had moved to Japan, invited me on the trip, and I was very impressed with the ramen, sushi, and other Japanese food. Both Sam and JJ were similarly impressed in Japan. The focus on dashi and umami in ramen, in particular, was something that one couldn't do at Chez Panisse, which is based on Italian-French cuisine.

S: And the way the Japanese concentrated on the ramen bowl in front of them, like a ritual, was very moving. The medley of noodles as the main dish plus side dish ingredients was a style not found in the United States, and, above all, I was hooked by the taste. I also found it fascinating that each region has different styles, with the local culture and history in the background. To begin with, the components of deliciousness in Japanese cuisine differ from those in Western cuisine. A different balance for a different palette. This felt new to me.

―ラーメンショップをはじめた時の周りの反応は？

S：シェ・パニースの同僚のうち、若い連中はみんな興奮していたね。彼らはラーメンが好きだったし。反対にベテラン勢はなぜシェ・パニース同様のイタリアンフレンチをやらないのか不思議がっていた。でも実際にオープンしたら3時間待ちの行列ができるほどの人気を得た。正直、それはまったく想像していなかった状況だった。

R：生産者との繋がりをシェ・パニースの頃と変わらずに生かすことできたのはよかったと思う。それに日本のコピーをするのではなく、カリフォルニアだからできること、自分たちの環境でしかできないことをやろうと目指して、それを形にすることができたと思う。

日本のコピーをするのではなく、カリフォルニアだからできること、自分たちの環境でしかできないことをやろうと目指して

How did people react when you started Ramen Shop?

S: All of my young colleagues at Chez Panisse were excited. They liked ramen. In contrast, the veterans wondered why I wasn't doing Italian-French like Chez Panisse. But it became so popular when it opened that people had to wait three hours. Frankly, that was a situation I had not imagined at all.

R: I am glad we could keep the connection with the producers alive as we did at Chez Panisse. We also aimed to do something that could only be done in California, something that could only be done in our own environment, rather than copying Japan. I think we were able to do that.

We also aimed to do something that could only be done
in California,

― お店に『タンポポ』のポスターを飾られていますね

S：これはただのラーメン映画じゃないからね。食、それに食にまつわる感覚や官能、そして愛について描かれた映画だと思う。だからお店でスタッフのために上映会を催したこともあるし、常連にはピクサーのスタッフもいるから、ピクサーに持っていって彼らと一緒に観たこともあるよ。この「ラーメンショップ」をはじめるためにアメリカでも日本でもラーメン屋をたくさんリサーチしたから、映画の中でタンポポがショーヘイと他のラーメン屋を偵察するシーンには共感したし、ギャングの男が死ぬ間際に猪の腸詰について語るシーンは最高だよね。とても先鋭的だったから、興奮せずにはいられなかった。

― レイさんにとって一番印象的だったシーンは？

R：危篤のお母さんが家族に焼き飯を作って亡くなるシーンだね。食べることとはつまり、家族を育てることでしょう。だから僕は家でも家族にご飯を作るんだ。この映画に限らず、日本で経験したことも含めて感じることは、「食べる」ことに対するリスペクト。日本人は食事の前に「いただきます」、食事のあとに「ごちそうさま」といって感謝の気持ちを表すでしょう？ ラーメン屋ならお店が混んでいればなるべく早く済ますようにするし。僕らも創業時お客さんに同じような対応を期待してしまったけど、なかなか難しいよね。おしゃべりを止めて、目の前のラーメンに集中してもらった方が絶対美味しい状態を楽しんでもらえるはずだけど、文化の違いであることをしばらくしてから理解できるようになった。

something that could only be done in our own environment, rather than copying Japan.

You have a poster of Tampopo in your shop.

S: It's not just a ramen film. It is a film about food, the sensations, and the sensuality associated with food and love. So I've hosted screenings for the staff at the store. Also, some of the regulars are Pixar staff, so I took the film to Pixar and watched it with them too. I researched a lot of ramen restaurants in both the U.S. and Japan to start Ramen Shop, so I connected with the scene in the movie where Tampopo scouts out other ramen shops with Shohei. I also love the scene where the gangster talks about boar sausage as he is about to die. It was so edgy, I couldn't help but get excited.

What was the most memorable scene for you, Ray?

R: The one where the critically ill mother makes fried rice for her family and then dies. Eating, in other words, is raising a family. That's why I cook for my family at home. What I feel, not only in this film but also in my experiences in Japan, is respect for "eating." Japanese people express gratitude by saying itadakimasu before meals and gochisosama after meals, right? Also, in ramen shops, people try to finish up as fast as possible if the restaurant is crowded. When we started our business, we expected our customers to do the same thing, but it didn't come easy. I came to understand after a while that it is a cultural difference, although it would surely be better for them to stop chatting and concentrate on the ramen so they can enjoy it tasting best.

―『タンポポ』同様に、お店のオープンをサポートしてくれた仲間がいましたか？

S：特定のひとりを挙げることは難しいけれど、設計士のワイリー・プライスは情熱を持って多くのことに対応してくれたよ。お店の設計のみならずバーの棚を取り付けてくれたり、本来の仕事の領域を超えてさまざまなことをやってくれた。

R：たくさんの助けがあったし、その多くは僕らの友達であり、コミュニティだった。ラーメンのどんぶりも、壁の装飾も見ず知らずの業者によるものじゃない。そして数多くの生産者たちが僕らを日々支えてくれているんだ。

―『タンポポ』のゴローやセンセイのように、これまでのキャリアで導いてくれた人は？

R：シェ・パニースで師事したラッセル・ムーアからは多くのことを学んだよ。自分のキャリアの中で知る限り最も難しい人だったと思うけれど、レシピに頼らず、直感で自分が求める味に近づいていくことを教えてくれた。彼がシェ・パニース後に経営していたカミノはその美学を実践していた素晴らしいレストランだったよ。

S：僕の場合は同じシェ・パニースでも、ワイン・ディレクターであるジョナサン・ウォーターズがメンターさ。彼は、いつだってどんな人でも温かく迎えていた。心からのおもてなし、ホスピタリティという意味を僕に教えてくれた恩人なんだ。

＊サンフランシスコでの取材から1ヶ月も経たぬうちに、
　ジョナサン氏が交通事故で他界する不幸に見舞われました。心よりご冥福をお祈りいたします。

We had so much help;
a lot of it was our friends and community.

Like in Tampopo, were there any people in your circle who helped you open Ramen Shop?

S: It's hard to name one particular person, but our architect, Wiley Price, handled a lot of things with enthusiasm. Not only did he design the store, but he did many things beyond his original work scope, like installing bar shelves.

R: We had so much help; a lot of it was our friends and community. Neither the ramen bowls nor the wall decorations were made by strangers. And numerous producers support us on a daily basis.

Who has guided you in your careers, like Goro and Sensei in Tampopo?

R: I learned a lot from Russell Moore, my mentor at Chez Panisse. He was probably the most difficult person I have known in my career, but he taught me not to rely on recipes and use my intuition to get closer to the flavor I wanted. The Camino, which he ran after leaving Chez Panisse, was a great restaurant that really lived up to that principle.

S: In my case, my mentor is Jonathan Waters,* the wine director at Chez Panisse. He always welcomed everyone warmly. I owe him a debt of gratitude for teaching me the meaning of hospitality from the heart.

*Less than a month after the interview in San Francisco, Waters sadly passed away in a traffic accident. May he rest in peace.

― シェフとして大事にしていることはなんでしょう？

R：シェフであり続けること、料理し続けることがなにより大切だと思う。パンデミック
の間によく考えたんだ。なぜ人は外に出掛けるのか？　辿り着いた答えは、人に出会うた
めなんだっていう当たり前のことだった。そのためにここに来て、そのために飲食を楽し
む。その時自分がシェフとして存在していられることが、なによりの歓びなんだ。

― ラーメンショップが社会に対して貢献していることは？

S：良きコミュニティとして存在していること。それが良いレストランとしての条件でも
あると思う。心地よくて安全で、健康的なコミュニティをみんなが求めているし、だから
こそ本来の繋がりを強制的に断たなければいけなかったパンデミックは本当に大変だっ
た。ましてや僕らのコミュニティは Food Hub Project の真鍋太一や eatrip の野村友里な
ど日本にも広がっている。海を超えても僕らは理解し合っているし、お互いを歓迎し合っ
ているんだ。

サム・ホワイト & レイニエル・デ・グズマン

カリフォルニア・オークランドでオーガニック料理の母と呼ばれるアリス・ウォータースが営むレストラン「シェ・パニース」
でキャリアを積んだ二人が、現在は日本を拠点とするベーカリー・シェフのジェリー・ジャクシッチ（JJ）と 2013 年に同じオー
クランドのロックリッジに「ラーメンショップ」を開業する。レイニエルはチーフ・シェフとして、サムはバーの責任者とし
てお店に立ち、日本のオーセンティックな手法と異なる卓越した発想で北カリフォルニアの食材をラーメンに翻訳し、現地の
食通たちを満足させている。

What is important to you as a chef?

R: I think the most important thing is to keep being a chef and keep cooking. I thought about it a lot during the pandemic. Why do people go out? The answer I arrived at was obvious: to meet people. That's why they come here, and that's why they enjoy eating and drinking. The greatest joy for me is to be able to be a chef at such moments.

What does Ramen Shop contribute to society?

S: Existing as a good community. I think that is a requirement for a good restaurant. We all want a comfortable, safe, and healthy community, and that's why the pandemic, which forced us to cut off our essential connections to others, was really hard. Furthermore, our community has expanded to Japan, including Taichi Manabe of the Food Hub Project and Yuri Nomura of eatrip. Even across the ocean, we understand and welcome each other.

Sam White & Rayneil De Guzman

After building their careers at Chez Panisse in Berkeley, California, the restaurant run by the mother of organic cuisine Alice Waters, the two opened Ramen Shop in Oakland's Rockridge neighborhood in 2013 with JJ (Jerry Jaksich), who is now based in Tokyo as a bakery chef. With Rayneil as chief chef and Sam in charge of the bar, they have been satisfying local foodies by translating Northern California ingredients into ramen with outstanding ideas not bound by authentic Japanese methods.

ERECTED A.D.1896
BY THE BOARD
– OF –
STATE HARBOR COMMISSIONERS

Holly Juliet Zimbert

Ben Bernthal

ホリー・ジュリエット・ジンバート

" eat , love , life "
GIVE 3 WORDS

Photographs_Makoto Miura

ERECTED A.D 1896
BY THE BOARD
OF
STATE HARBOR COMMISSIONERS

オークランドのラーメンショップでサムとレイの取材を終え、ファーマーズマーケットで賑わう週末のフェリービルディングに向かうと、はじめて見かける"生産者"に出会った。彼らのブースに並ぶのは野菜でも果物でもなく、2台のヴィンテージ・タイプライター。

そう。ホリーとベンの二人は採れたての詩をお裾分けしてくれるのだ。種はこちらが提供する3つのキーワード。生産期間は30分。行列のフードトラック ROLI ROTI でポルケッタ・サンドを頰張っている間に、今回はホリーがこの本のために特別な詩を用意してくれた。

After interviewing Sam and Ray at their ramen shop in Oakland, I went to the Ferry Building for the weekend Farmer's Market, where I first encountered "the producers." At their booth I found, not fruits and vegetables, but rather two vintage typewriters.

Yes. Holly and Ben cultivate poetry to share with others. You supply three keywords that are the seed. Time to harvest is 30 minutes. While I was stuffing my face with a porchetta sandwich from Roli Roti, a nearby food truck, Holly prepared a special poem for this book.

The palate expands from sheltering
the tongue
to
showcasing its senses.

Acidity aligns in awakening
a savory notion
sparks the slow
moving
of comfort.

We eat, when we land our eyes
upon the feasting & offering--
that
is
love.

Today, I gaze into my bowl & slurp
the day like
ramen.
" eat, love, life "   For Colaxo
San Francisco, CA

-Holly Juliet Zimbert   @pussycroc
hollyjulietzimbert.com

ラーメンのような
その日を
食べる、愛、　そして人生
コラクソーへ
サンフランシスコのホリー・ジュリエット・ジンバート

ホリー・ジュリエット・ジンバート
詩人／マルチメディアアーティスト

オリジナルの抽象水彩画に詩をタイプする作品を携え、米国中を旅している。街角や公園、または結婚式、マーケット、フェスティバルに企業パーティーなど、様々なイベントで詩を披露。これらの創作活動に加え、カリグラフィーや招待状、ペーパーグッズの創作にアート作品の依頼も受けている。

味覚は拡がる

舌を手繰り寄せ

神経を奮わせて

酸味は香ばしさを呼び覚まし

心地よい感情が

緩やかに弾ける

わたしたちは食べる

愛そのものと言える

ご馳走や捧げものが

目の前に　現れたとき

そして今日

わたしはどんぶりを見つめ　啜る

Holly Juliet Zimbert
Poet / Multimedia Artist

She travels around the country, typing custom poetry onto original abstract watercolor paintings. She does this on street corners and in parks, as well as during highly-curated events. In addition to custom poetry, Holly also creates custom calligraphy, event invitations and paper goods as well as commissioned works of art.

謙遜の美徳

Modesty as a virtue

 Photograph_Tetsuya Ito   Cooking & Styling_Yuri Nomura (eatrip)

Words of Outsiders

3

ボーイ　「こちら様は？」

専務　「僕も、舌平目」

ボーイ　「スープかサラダはお付け致しましょうか？」

専務　「コンソメ。サラダは、要らないや」

Waiter	For you, sir?
Salaryman	I'll have the sole too.
Waiter	Soup or salad, sir?
Salaryman	Consommé. No salad.

表裏一体の
新旧、真贋、
ドラマが生む深み

青野賢一

映画『タンポポ』が劇場公開されたのは1985年（昭和60年）。日本では1973年のオイルショックで経済成長率が鈍化し、高度経済成長は終わりを迎えるものの、1980年代に入ると経常収支はおもに外需主導で黒字化する。日本の自動車産業と電子・電機機器産業は世界市場を席巻し、なかでも一番の貿易相手国であったアメリカは輸入超過で大きなダメージを受けていた。いわゆる日米貿易摩擦である。こうしたなかで、過度なドル高を是正し、ドル安誘導を行うことで相対的にアメリカの輸出競争力を高めるという内容の「プラザ合意」がなされたのが1985年。このプラザ合意は日本国内では円高不況の懸念から低金利政策の継続をもたらし、1986年終盤からのバブル経済を準備するひとつのきっかけとなった。

バブルに突入する前まで、日本は安定成長期と呼ばれる状況にあった。「1970年代から80年代にかけては、消費者物価の大幅な上昇がみられる一方、現金給与総額はそれ以上に上昇しており、実質賃金が上昇していた」「実質賃金の上昇は人々の購買力を高め、消費を刺激し経済成長に寄与するだけでなく、生活に豊かさをもたらすことになる」（いずれも厚生労働省「平成23年版　労働経済の分析」第二章「経済社会の

推移と世代ごとにみた働き方」）。簡単にいうと、バブル期ほどではないにせよ好景気ムードがあり、少なくない数の人々が豊かな生活を享受していた、軽度の躁状態とでもいうような社会状況が『タンポポ』の頃の日本、特に東京を筆頭とする都市圏にはあったのだ。こうした時代背景を頭に入れつつ、『タンポポ』のなかの、会社役員たちのフランス料理店での昼食という挿話をひもといてみよう。

「ラーメン屋は体力だ！」というゴローの考えからランニングに勤しむタンポポ。ひと通り走り終えて呼吸を整える整理体操をしていると、スーツ姿、というよりは背広姿といった男たちがタンポポとゴローの横を通り抜ける。男たちは6人。専務、常務と管理職合わせて5人、そしてその後ろに役員たちのカバンを持たされた平社員（加藤賢崇）が続く。彼らが向かうのは高級ホテルのなかにある高級フレンチの店である。シーフードが有名だというその店の個室に入り、役員たちと同じタイミングで着席しようとする平社員の首根っこをつかまえて「お前はまだだ！」とでもいうように無言でたしなめる管理職のひとり。ウエイター（橋爪功）が皆にメニューを配る。「お決まりでございましょうか？」

The Depth Created by Inextricably Linked New and Old, Authentic and False, and Drama

Kenichi Aono

The motion picture *Tampopo* was released in theaters in 1985. Although the oil shock of 1973 had slowed Japan's economic growth rate and the post-war economic miracle was heading towards its end, foreign demand led Japan's current-account balance into the black as the country moved into the 1980s. Japanese automobiles, along with electronic and electrical machinery industries, took world markets by storm, causing significant damage to the country's largest trading partner, the United States. Out of this so-called Japan-U.S. trade friction came the Plaza Accord in 1986, which sought to correct the excessively high appreciation of the U.S. dollar and bring its value down against other currencies to make American exports more competitive. Concerns over a "high-yen recession" in the domestic Japanese economy led the government to continue a policy of low-interest rates, which helped trigger the "bubble" economy that began to develop late in 1986.

Before Japan rushed into that bubble, it was in a period of stable growth. "From the 1970s into the 1980s, while there was a large increase in consumer prices, there was even larger growth in total cash earnings and a rise in real wages." "Not only does the rise in real wages increase purchasing power, contributing to economic growth by stimulating consumption, but it also makes people more affluent." (Both quotes are from "The Transition to an Economic Society and Work Methods as Seen by each Generation," Chapter 2 of the Ministry of Health, Labour and Welfare's "2011 Analysis of Labour Economy,") To put it simply, while it was not on the level of the bubble era, when *Tampopo* was released, there was a mood of prosperity, particularly in Tokyo and other urban areas, and a social situation that can be described as mildly manic, with more than a few people enjoying a more affluent lifestyle. With this historical background in mind, let us look into the episode in *Tampopo*, where corporate executives and others have lunch at a French restaurant.

Goro's claim that "Ramen shop-owners have stamina" encourages the ramen restaurant owner Tampopo to take up running. After she has run for a distance and is doing calisthenics to stabilize her breathing, some men wearing suits, or more accurately suits wearing men, pass beside her and Goro. There are six of them. An executive director, managing director, and three managers account for five, while bringing up the rear, charged with carrying their briefcases, is a young rank-and-file employee (Kenso Kato). Their destination is the high-class French restaurant in a high-class hotel. They

専務は「う、うん……さぁねぇ……」、常務は「私は
まだあんまりお腹が空いていないから、何か軽いもの
を」という返答。ふたりともフランス語で書かれたメ
ニューを理解できずに決められないのだ。続いて管理
職のひとりがウエイターに声をかけ、舌平目のムニエ
ルを注文する。「スープかサラダはお付けしますか？」
と問われコンソメ・スープを、飲み物は「ビール。ハ
イネケンある？」とオーダー。それを見て先の専務、
常務もまるっきり同じ内容で注文する。ほかの2名の管
理職も当然ながら同様だ。そして最後に平社員。目上
の人に謙虚に従うのが普通であるこの時代の――そ
して現代でも往々にしてみられる――考え方から、
その場にいる誰もが同じ注文をすると思っていたら、
なんと彼はメニューをまじまじと眺め「クネールかぁ
……この《クネールのブーダン風》っていうのはクネー
ルをブーダンのかたちに作ったってこと？」とウエイ
ターに質問する。「左様でございます」とウエイター。
ちなみに「クネール」と発音しているが、これは「ク
ネル」のことで、すり潰した白身魚を球形や円筒形に
した、日本でいう「つみれ」のようなもの。「ブーダン」
は確かフランスの「タイユヴァン」で同じものを出し
ていたと思うと平社員がいうと、ウエイターは感心してこのレストランのシェフ
は豚の血と脂の腸詰である。

ちなみに「クネール」と発音しているが、これは「ク
ネル」のことで、すり潰した白身魚を球形や円筒形に
した、日本でいう「つみれ」のようなもの。「ブーダン」
は豚の血と脂の腸詰である。

は「タイユヴァン」で修行したのだと返した。最終的
に平社員は《クネールのブーダン風》メインに《エ
スカルゴのパイ詰》、それから《くるみとりんごのサ
ラダ》、そしてワインの銘柄と年まで指定というパー
フェクトなオーダーをウエイターに告げるのだった。
その様子を見ていた役員や管理職の顔は全員真っ赤。
文字通り赤っ恥をかかされたわけである。

この時代には、それまでの価値観では理解が追いつ
かない自由な発想と新しい生活様式を持った若者を指
す「新人類」という言葉が流行したが、前述の平社員
はまさにその新人類の代表格として描かれている。空
気を読まず、多数派に流されない。物質的豊かさが当
たり前の環境で育ち、教養もある。そんな彼がとった
行動が会社でのヒエラルキーをたちどころに逆転させ
てしまうのである。自分より地位の高い人や年長者に
接するときの「謙遜」という本来ならば美しい態度が、
実はアイデンティティの放棄と表裏一体である事実を
本作はまざまざと突きつける。そのことと新人類たる
平社員の唯我独尊さとの対比が観る者の笑いを誘うの
だが、ふと「はて、自分はどうだろうか？」と考えさ
せられるところに深みや批評性を感じられはしないだ
ろうか。

enter a private dining room in this establishment, apparently known for its seafood. When the young employee goes to seat himself at the same time as the executives, one of the managers grabs him by the back of his jacket as if to silently say, "You wait!" The waiter (Isao Hashizume) passes out menus to all. The names of the dishes are in French. To the question, "Are you ready to order?" the executive director responds with, "Uh...hmm," while the managing director answers, "I'm not very hungry yet, so perhaps something light." Since neither can read the French on the menu, they are unable to decide. One of the managers speaks to the waiter, ordering sole meunière. Asked "Would you like soup or salad?" he asks for consommé soup and then orders "Beer. Do you have Heineken?" Seeing this, the Executive and Managing directors order exactly the same thing. The other two managers follow suit as if this were only natural. Finally comes the young rank-and-file employee. In the custom of that time—one still often seen today—when the normal thing to do would be to meekly follow the lead of his superiors and anybody in that situation would be expected to order the same thing, he surprises everyone by looking seriously at the menu and asking the waiter, "'Quenelle'? Is that quenelle au boudin? A dumpling shaped like a sausage?" "Yes, sir," says the waiter. In addition, while it is pronounced to sound like "QueNELLE," it is in fact "QUEnelle", mashed white fish formed into a spherical or cylindrical shape in a dish resembling Japanese *tsumire* fish dumplings. "Boudin" is a sausage of pork blood and fat. When the young employee says he believes the same dish is served at the restaurant "Taillevent," the waiter answers in an admiring tone that the chef here trained at that famous Parisian establishment. In the end the young employee announces a perfect order to the waiter of quenelle au boudin, an escargot pie main dish, a walnut and apple salad, and a wine order complete down to brand and year. The faces of the watching executives and managers are bright red. They have been deeply humiliated.

At this time, the expression "new breed" was common in describing young people whose concept of freedom and new lifestyle were incomprehensible to those with the values that had prevailed until then. The young employee is definitely envisioned as a representative of this type: unaware of his proper place or of the need to go along with the majority. This type of person has been raised in an environment where richness in material things was taken for granted, but with a sense of culture. His action comprises a reversal then and there of the company

さて、『タンポポ』の時代背景は冒頭に記したとおりだが、バブル期直前というこの頃の日本、東京の特異性が物語に絶妙な味わいを与えているのを忘れてはならない。その特異性とは、新しいものと古いもの、高級なものと庶民的なもの、本物とうわべだけのものといった事柄がぎりぎり共存——先の挿話ではないが表裏一体といってもいい——している点である。さまざまなことがマニュアル化、カタログ化されて誰でも「おいしい店」や「そこで何をオーダーするのがベスト」かを知ることができ、また地上げによるスクラップ＆ビルドが急速に進行し古い家屋が新しい高層ビルディングに変わってしまうバブル期ではこうはいかない。フランス料理店で赤っ恥をかかされたお偉いさんたちは、きっと1年後にはワインの蘊蓄のひとつも傾けているだろう。そこに至る前、本物＝平社員とうわべだけの人＝会社の偉い人が同じテーブルに着いて、前者が後者のメッキをいとも簡単に剥がしてしまうところに痛快さがあるわけである。これと同じようなおかしみは、ホームレスたちがすこぶるグルメだというシークエンスにも見てとれるだろう。

新しいものと古いもの、高級なものと庶民的なものが表裏一体で共存していることを先に述べたが、「表

裏一体」という部分に着目すると、メインストーリーであるタンポポとゴローたちの物語と、一見それとは無関係そうなサイドストーリーは実はすぐ近くで起こっていることが少なくない。トレーニングしているタンポポたちのそばを通って6人の男たちが徒歩で向かった件のフレンチレストランはホテルに入っており、同じフロアでは「スパゲッティの食べ方講座」が催され、ウエイターは粋な格好の男女が泊まるホテルの部屋にルームサービスを運ぶ。これ以外の挿話でもメインとサブは地理的な接点が少なからずあって、それはいわば表通りと裏通りの関係のようなものだ。「タンポポ・ラーメン」成功への物語のすぐそばで、人は恥をかき、卵黄を口移しし、銃弾に倒れ、窃盗で逮捕され、病で死んでゆく——。こうしてみてゆくと、『タンポポ』に複雑で奥行きのある魅力をもたらしているのは、社会のおかしさや人生の悲哀を感じさせるサイドストーリーであることは間違いなさそうだ。

青野賢一（あおの・けんいち）
文筆家／選曲家

株式会社ビームスにて PR、クリエイティブ・ディレクター、BEAMS RECORDS のディレクターなどを務めた後、2021年独立。音楽、ファッション、映画、文学、美術といった文化芸術全般をフィールドにした文筆家、DJ、選曲家として活躍している。近著に『音楽とファッション　6つの現代的視点』（リットーミュージック、2022年）。

hierarchy. This work clearly forces on us the reality that on the other side of the coin from the purity of attitude traditionally represented as "humility" in relation to social superiors or elders is the relinquishing of one's own identity. The comparison with the egotism of this new breed of young person may invite the scorn of watchers, but at a deeper and more critical level, are we not suddenly forced to stop and think, "Well then, what about me?"

While I have noted the historical background, we must not forget the unique aspect of Japan and Tokyo in this period just before the bubble that gives this story its exquisite flavor. This special quality is a reluctant coexistence—a different coin from the one mentioned above but two-sided nonetheless—of the new and the old, the high class and the common, and the real and the superficial. This would no longer apply in the era of the bubble when growing reliance on manuals and catalogs for various things made it possible for anyone to search out "a good place to eat" and "the best thing to order," while a scrap-and-build policy caused by rising land prices saw old housing replaced by high-rise buildings. Within a year, the embarrassed executives in the French restaurant would very probably have a vast knowledge of wine upon which to draw. But before that point is reached, there is the thrill of watching as the connoisseur—the young employee—reveals the true colors of the pretenders—the managers. A similar humor can be seen in the sequence involving the homeless who turn out to be discerning gourmets.

We have said how the new and the old, and the high-class and the common, exist together as two sides of the same coin, but if we focus on this "two-sidedness," the main story of Tampopo and Goro, as well as the sub-stories that at first glance have little connection with it, are in fact occurring very close to each other in more than a few ways. The French restaurant to which the six men are headed when they walk past Tampopo and Goro is in a hotel, on the same floor of which a "How to Eat Spaghetti Seminar" is being held, and meanwhile, on another floor, a waiter is taking room service to a stylishly dressed man and woman. There are more than a few instances in which these main and side stories intersect geographically in a relation similar to a main street and back alleys. Close beside the "Tampopo Ramen" success story, people are embarrassed, an egg yolk passes from mouth to mouth, a man is shot down, a thief is caught, and there is a death of disease... Seen this way, it would seem that the strangeness of society and the pathos of life in the side stories cause us to feel bring about the complicated depth of the film's appeal.

Translation_Ian MacDougall

Kenichi Aono
Writer / Music Director

Aono became an independent writer/director in 2021 after being responsible for BEAMS Co., Ltd.'s public relations and working as a director for BEAMS RECORDS. Active in culture and the arts as a writer, DJ, and musical director, his activities include music, fashion, film, literature, and the fine arts. His most recent publication is *Music and Fashion: Six Contemporary Perspectives* (Rittor Music, Inc., 2022)

ホテルメトロポリタンエドモント（飯田橋）
Hotel Metropolitan Edmont, IIDABASHI

サラリーマン一行のビジネスランチ会場は、当時のフランス料理店から現在は中華料理店に。ホテル内に出店している中国料理の老舗「南国酒家」、その個室である「胡蝶蘭」の壁面に、映画と変わらぬ意匠を確認できる。

The businessmen gather for lunch in what then served French food, but is now a Chinese restaurant. The walls of the private room "Kochoran," of the long-established Chinese restaurant "Nangokushuka" located in the hotel, are the same design as when the movie was filmed.

Photograph_Tetsuya Ito   Cooking & Styling_Yuri Nomura (eatrip)

規 律 と 崩 壊
Discipline & Disruption

「この場合大切なことは、決して音を立てないことです」

「ぜったいに音を立ててはいけません！」

Words of Outsiders

The most important thing

is not to make any noise.

You absolutely must not make any noise !

「ごった煮の原理」

鍵和田啓介

　日本人よ、これがホンモノだ。

　何よりもまずそれを打ち出したことが、1960年代後半にエッセイストとして頭角を現した伊丹十三の新しさだった。外国文化を自分勝手にアレンジして受容する日本人を軽妙洒脱にディスり、自身がヨーロッパで見聞してきたホンモノを伝導することでもって、一世を風靡したのだった。槍玉に挙げられる話題は、グルメからファッションまで多岐に渡ったが、とりわけ伊丹が執着していたのがスパゲッティである。「スパゲッティのおいしい召し上がり方」(『女たちよ！』)という文章には、概ね次のようなことが綴られている。

　外国の文明を輸入するには二つの方法がある。包容型と吸収型である。日本人は頑固な吸収型である。しかも、とても貧しい後進的な吸収型である。日本における麺を茹ですぎたスパゲッティを見れば一目瞭然だ。それはスパゲッティの名を借りた炒め餛飩でしかない。イタリア人が理想とする麺の硬さ、すなわち「アル・デンテ」すらも知らない。加えて、なにゆえ日本人はスパゲッティに鶏やハムや海老やマッシュルームを入れてケチャップで和えるようなことをするのか。しからば、ホンモノのスパゲッティの作り方を教えてしんぜよう。といった具合である。

The Principle of Hodgepodge

Keisuke Kagiwada

"Japanese people, this is the real thing."

To begin with, it was before anything else the novelty with which Juzo Itami burst upon the scene as an essayist in the late 1960s. Having been to Europe and seen its authentic culture for himself, he took the world by storm, mocking with a light and stylish touch those Japanese who took in that foreign culture in such a way as to suit it to themselves. A wide range was exposed to his ridicule, from gourmet dining to high fashion, but in particular, it was spaghetti upon which he fastened. In his essay "How to Eat Spaghetti so it Tastes Best," from his collection entitled *Listen, Women!* he spells out

something that goes roughly as follows.

"There are two ways of incorporating foreign civilization: encapsulation and absorption. Japanese are stubborn absorptionists. And they are poor, backward absorptionists. This is obvious at a glance when one sees their overboiled spaghetti. This is nothing more than fried udon noodles borrowing the name of spaghetti. The Japanese do not even know the hardness of spaghetti, called 'al dente,' that Italians hold up as an ideal. And as well, why do the Japanese put chicken, ham, shrimp, or mushrooms into their spaghetti and then garnish it

伊丹が伝導するのは、ホンモノのスパゲッティの作り方だけに留まらず、食べ方にも及ぶ。「スパゲッティの正しい食べ方」(『ヨーロッパ退屈日記』)というエッセイでは、右手に持ったフォークに2、3本の麺をひっかけ、ときに左手に持ったスプーンの窪みを使いつつそれを巻ききり、音を立てずに啜るといったことが懇切丁寧に語られる。

では、『タンポポ』の劇中、高級レストランの席上において、岡田茉莉子演じる講師が女性生徒たちにスパゲッティ・アレ・ボンゴレの食べ方を、スプーンとフォークを使った麺の巻取り方に至るまでを指導する「スパゲッティの召し上がり方講座」のシークエンスは、一連のエッセイのセルフリメイクなのだろうか。のちの展開を鑑みるに、そこまで単純ではない。なぜなら、その光景を遠くの席で見守っていた外国人(一説にはフランス人のパティシエらしい)が、最初こそその作法に真似ようとするも、すぐに放棄してズルズルと汚い音を立てながらスパゲッティを啜り始めるからだ。しかも、生徒たちもこれに共鳴するように、ズルズルと啜り始める。結果、レストランには常軌を逸したズルズル音が横溢することになるのだが、伊丹が伝導したホンモノの作法がまるっきり無視されているのは明らかだろう。この事態をどう受け止めるべきか。

本作を彩るいくつかの挿話がヒントになりそうだ。そこでは食にまつわるあれこれを通して、ルールを逸脱することの快楽が描かれている。甘いおやつを禁じられているのにソフトクリームを頬張る男児、食事制限されているのに無視する老人などがそれに当たる。伊丹の監督第1作であり、『タンポポ』の前作にあたる『お葬式』が、お葬式というセレモニーにおいて、ガチガチに固められたルールを遵守しようとする者たちの滑稽さを描いていたことを思うと、この事態はなかなか興味深い。ともあれ、『タンポポ』の主題である「食欲」は、ときに命懸けであっても、ルールを踏み越えさせてしまう力を持っているということだろう。スパゲッティのズルズル食べにしても同じである。実際、一心不乱にズルズル啜る者たちは、さながら「食欲」によって駆動する自動人形のごとき気迫を湛えている。

いやいや、あれほどホンモノ由来のルールを重んじた伊丹のことだから、ここには外国人に感化されやすい日本人への皮肉を読み取るべきではないか。そんな意見が聞こえてきそうだし、一理あるかもしれない。しかし、伊丹がディスり続けた日本人による外国文化の輸入形態を、ルールを無視したオリジナルと日本的なものの「ごった煮」と言い換えるなら、『タンポポ』

with ketchup? In that case, let us do them the service of teaching them how to prepare real spaghetti."

What Itami conveys to us does not stop with how to make real spaghetti; he goes on to include how to eat it. In an essay called "The Correct Way to Eat Spaghetti" from his *Diary of Boredom in Europe*, he explains with great care how to snare two or three strands with a fork held in the right hand and then how to roll these in the bowl of a spoon held in the left, and how to draw this silently into the mouth.

So in the movie *Tampopo*, when the instructor played by Mariko Okada in the "How to Eat Spaghetti Seminar" sequence is teaching the female students in a high-class restaurant how to eat spaghetti alle vongole, even down to how to use the fork and spoon to wind the noodles, is he remaking a series of his own essays? Considering how things develop, it is not that simple. This is because a foreigner (in fact a French pâtissier Anbré Lecomte) watching over the scene from a distant table starts out seemingly imitating this way of eating but quickly abandons it and begins slurping his spaghetti with a vulgar noise. The students too, as if in sympathy, begin to slurp. As a result, the restaurant is flooded with bizarre slurping sounds, and it is obvious that Itami is completely ignoring the proper etiquette

here. How should we accept this?

The side stories that garnish the film seem to provide a hint. Through the various ways in which the film connects to food, it portrays the pleasure of breaking the rules. Illustrating this is a little boy forbidden to snack on sweet things who devours a soft serve ice cream cone and an elderly man who ignores his dietary restrictions. This becomes deeply interesting when considering *The Funeral*, Itami's first film and the one that precedes *Tampopo*, which portrays the absurdity of people trying to follow the hard-and-fast rules governing a funeral ceremony. At any rate, "appetite," the main theme of *Tampopo*, has the power to make people break the rules, even if sometimes at the risk of their lives. This is the same with slurping spaghetti. Those people so intently slurping are exactly like automata driven by their appetites.

But wait. Since this is the Itami who adheres so strongly to authentic rules, can this not be understood as sarcasm towards Japanese who are so easily impressed by foreigners? This seems like an opinion one might hear, and it may have some truth. However, if we take the way that foreign culture is imported into Japan, of which Itami is critical throughout, and call that way a "hodgepodge" combining something Japanese and a foreign original

がそのごった煮の原理にこそ貫かれているのは、どうしたことか。

そもそもメインストーリーの重要アイテムであるラーメンからして、スパゲッティと同じく外国料理である日本的なもののごった煮に他ならない。また、そのメインストーリーが、『シェーン』をはじめとする西部劇の典型的な物語を翻案した「ラーメンウエスタン」であることは、伊丹自身も語っている通りだ。しかも、その合間には、ルイス・ブニュエル監督作『自由の幻想』に着想を得たという、本筋から逸脱した挿話が縦横無尽に組み込まれる。作品の大枠だけ見ても、ごった煮のオンパレードだ。

細部に目を凝らしても事情は同じである。「スパゲッティの召し上がり方講座」のシークエンスについて言えば、例の常軌を逸したズルズル音は、現実にスパゲッティを啜るときの音とは明らかに異なる。ある行為にその自然音とは異なるニセモノの音を当てるというのも、ごった煮の一例と言えるだろう。

映画はニセモノ的で、ごった煮的で、ルール無用の芸術である。カメラが映せるのは現実の似姿でしかないし、映像や音響をはじめとするさまざまな要素が入り乱れているし、打ち立てられたルールは常に更

新され続けて今に至る。そのことを、伊丹が知らなかったはずがない。伊丹はそんな映画に魅せられた自身も手を染めるにあたり、あれほどディスっていた日本人のごった煮的な性質との相性の良さを感知し、面白がりつつあったのではないか。映画を作り始めたのときと同じくして、かつてのヨーロッパ的なホンモノのファッションから、チャイナジャケットの上に刺し子の半纏を羽織るごった煮なそれへと変化していった伊丹の姿を見るにつけ、あながち的外れでもないような気がしてくる。

鍵和田啓介（かぎわだ・けいすけ）
ライター

映画批評家であり、「爆音映画祭」のディレクターである樋口泰人氏に誘われ、大学時代よりライター活動を開始。現在は『POPEYE』『BRUTUS』などの雑誌を中心に、さまざまな記事を執筆している。著書に『みんなの映画100選』。

whose rules are ignored, how is it that *Tampopo* is carried out precisely on the principle of such hodgepodge?

In the first place, ramen, the main item in the story, is like spaghetti, a kind of hodgepodge, a foreign dish done over in Japanese style. As Itami himself has said, *Tampopo* is a "ramen western" adapted from classic western movies such as *Shane*. And woven through this are anecdotes that deviate from the main storyline in every direction, inspired by director Luis Buñuel's film *The Phantom of Liberty*. Going from the film's framework, this is "hodgepodge" front and center.

With a close focus on details, the situation is still the same. The "How to Eat Spaghetti Seminar" sequence, with its bizarre slurping, is clearly very different from the sound when one eats spaghetti in reality. Applying a fake sound to an action so different from the natural sound can be another example of this "hodgepodge."

A motion picture is fake, a hodgepodge, an art form in which rules are futile. What the camera shows is no more than an imitation of reality, in which images, sound, and various other elements are jumbled together following rules that have constantly been revised right up to the present day.

Itami most certainly knew this. Films fascinated Itami, and when he tried his hand at making them, did he not sense that the hodgepodge character of the Japanese people he was mocking had an affinity with filmmaking, and go on to find amusement there? Seeing Itami at the time he took up making movies, changing from his former authentic European style of dress to the hodgepodge of a quilted hanten half-coat over a Chinese jacket, I feel this is not completely off the mark.

Translation_Ian MacDougall

Keisuke Kagiwada
Writer

A movie critic who began writing as a university student at the invitation of *Bakuon Film Festival* founder Yasuhito Higuchi. Kagiwada mainly writes magazine articles for publications such as *POPEYE* and *BRUTUS*. He is the author of *100 Movies for Everyone*.

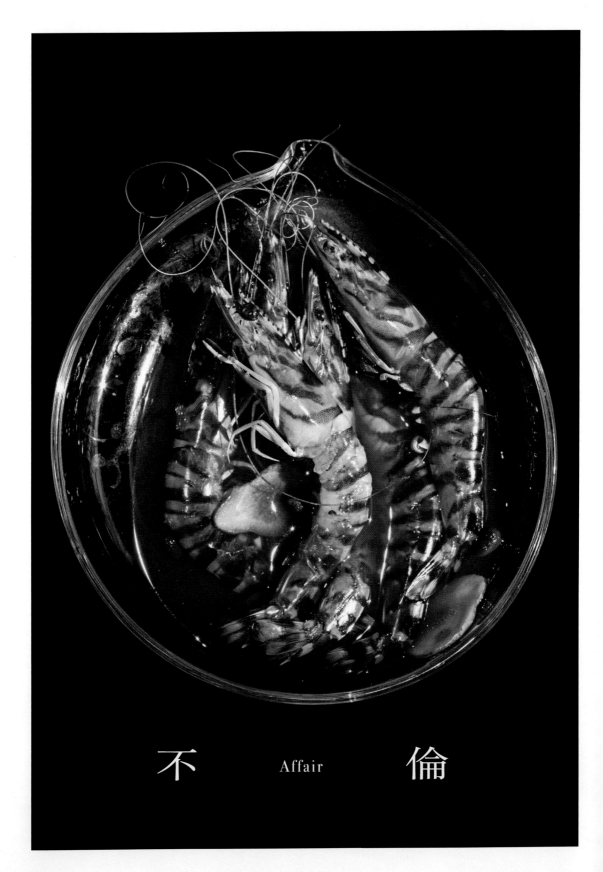

不　Affair　倫

Photograph_Tetsuya Ito

Cooking & Styling_Yuri Nomura (eatrip)

A hotel rooms

moll's laughter

drunken shrimp dance on her belly

Words of Outsiders

○ ホテルの部屋

情婦の笑い声

酔っ払い海老が彼女の腹の上で踊る

「昼間の情事」

林 伸次

僕がバーテンダー修業をしていた頃のこと。たまにいらっしゃる中年のカップルがいまして、僕がてっきりご夫婦だと思ってお話ししていたら、あるとき「私たち夫婦じゃないですよ」と言われたことがありました。

後でバーテンダーの師匠の中村悌二さんに、「おまえなあ。夫婦は普通バーには来ないの。夫婦で今日はご飯作るの面倒くさいから居酒屋でとか、たまにレストランとかは行くよ。でもバーには行かないって。とくに日本はね。夫婦が暗くてロマンティックな場所でわざわざ高い酒を飲むわけないじゃない。夫婦が酒を飲みたかったら家で飲むんだよ。ましてや東京ならバーで夫婦に見えても不倫カップルってことよくあるから」と教えてもらいました。そういう事情って大人にならないとわからないものですよね。「バーで不倫カップルをお断りにしたら売り上げが四割落ちる」という都市伝説もあるほどです。これ、もちろんバーのお客様の四割が不倫カップルというわけではないんです。さすがにもうちょっと少ないはずです。ただ、不倫をしている人たちって、その恋愛の瞬間に非日常を求めているんじゃないかと思うのです。

お客さんの中には、「既婚女性専門」というとんでもなく悪い既婚男性がいまして、お互いが既婚同士だ

Love in the Afternoon

Shinji Hayashi

This happened when I was training to be a bartender. A middle-aged couple came in occasionally and, convinced they were man and wife, I would talk to them as such until one day they told me, "We're not married, you know."

Later, my bartending mentor Teiji Nakamura told me, "Oh, come on! Married couples don't usually go to bars. A married couple might decide they can't be bothered cooking today and go to a Japanese-style pub or something, or once in a while, they'll go to a restaurant. But they won't go to a bar. Especially Japanese. There's no way a married couple would deliberately drink expensive alcohol in a dark, romantic place. If they want to drink, they'll drink at home. To say nothing of the fact that what looks like a married couple in a Tokyo bar is often two people having an affair." You wouldn't know something like that until you had grown up, would you? This is so true that an urban legend says a bar that refuses service to unfaithful couples will see its sales fall by 40 percent. Of course, this does not mean that 40 percent of a bar's customers are couples cheating on their spouses. That figure must be a little less. However, I think in that instant of passion, those who are being unfaithful are probably seeking the thrill of the extraordinary.

と、お互い自分の家族を大切にしているから絶対にバレないようにしようってすごく注意をするし、向こうから「奥さんと別れて」なんてことも言ってこない、というのが彼の理屈でした。

その彼が、ある日ほろ酔い加減でグラスを傾けながら、「既婚女性をベッドにまで誘う方法」というのを語ってくれました。都内のちょっと良いホテルで、夜に食べると三万円くらいする、お寿司屋さんが、昼のランチだったら五千円くらいっていうのがありますよね。あれに既婚女性を誘うんだそうです。LINEでそのお寿司屋さんのURLを送信して「ここでランチでもどうですか?」って誘うと、美味しいお寿司なんて久しぶりだってことで、まあ来てくれるそうです。それで彼女とホテルの入り口で昼の十二時頃に待ち合わせをして、ビールなんかを飲みながらそのお寿司を食べますよね。その後、そのホテルのラウンジに移動しまして、シャンパーニュが飲めそうなんです。それでお互いちょっと酔っ払ってきて良い雰囲気になってきたときに、「このホテルの部屋、とってあるんだけど、そっちに移動しない?」って誘うのが彼の常套手段らしいのです。

これ、同じことを例えば銀座のお寿司屋さんでビール飲みながらランチのとしますよね。そうするとビールを飲みながら

お寿司を食べて、次にシャンパーニュが飲める銀座のカフェに歩いて移動しなきゃいけないんです。彼女ついてきてはくれないでしょう。あるいはタクシーに乗ってまでついてきてくれるでしょうか。まあカフェでシャンパーニュは飲めたとして、その後、予約しているホテルまで一緒に歩いて移動しなきゃ。外は明るいし、普通の人たちがいっぱいいる日常に、道中十分なほど触れてしまうわけですから。

でもそれが最初っからホテルの中なら、ちょっと薄暗いし、ホテルの中って常に非日常的だし、移動も全部エレベーターという個室だから妙な親密感も演出されて、成功率はまあグッと上がるそうなんです。その後、ホテルの部屋でまあ色々とあったとしても、夕方五時には彼女を新宿の小田急線(京王線でも埼京線でもいいですよ)には乗せられるから、彼女も安心なんだとか。

さて、映画『タンポポ』で白服の男が情婦が酔っ払い海老を食べるシーンですが、これ、パスタズルズルの後の「昼間のシーン」だということはお気づきでしょうか。この映画、僕は確か二十歳の頃にレンタルビデオを借りて観たのですが、この白服の男と情婦の意味だけがよくわからなかったんです。だいたい、なんで正装して昼間のホテルで会って、ルームサービスで料

Among my customers is a bad guy, a married man who specializes in dating married women. He reasons that if both are married, their families will be very important to them, and they will both be very careful that they are not found out, and his date will not say, "Leave your wife" or anything like that.

This man, tilting his glass one day when he was slightly drunk, told me his way of "getting a married woman into bed." A sushi restaurant at a somewhat posh downtown hotel will cost about 30,000 yen for dinner but only about 5,000 yen for lunch. That's where he would invite a married woman. When he sends the restaurant URL on the Line app with an invitation saying, "How about lunch here?" it will have been a while since she's had good sushi, and apparently, she'll come. He arranges to meet her at the hotel entrance around noon, and over a few beers, they'll have a sushi lunch. Afterward, they move to the hotel lounge and drink champagne or something. And then, after they're both a little drunk and in a good mood, he makes his usual move, saying, "I've taken a room in this hotel. Should we move there?"

Let's say you do the same thing at, for example, a sushi restaurant in Ginza. You drink beer while having a sushi lunch, and then next, you have to move, walking to a Ginza café where you can drink champagne. Will she come along with you? Anyway, even if she drinks champagne at the café, she probably won't walk with you, or even take a taxi, to the hotel room you've reserved. It's still bright outside, and you'll bump into a street full of ordinary people going about their ordinary day.

But suppose you're in a hotel from the very start. In that case, the lighting is dim, the interior is different from your everyday life, a strange feeling of intimacy comes into play when you enter that private room called an elevator, and your success rate leaps. After that, whatever may happen in the hotel room, at 5 p.m., she can get on the Odakyu Line train at Shinjuku Station (the Keio Line or the Saitama Line will also do fine), so she feels secure.

Now, have you noticed that the *Tampopo* scene in which the man in the white suit and his lover get drunk and eat shrimp, follows the slurping pasta sequence and is in the afternoon? I rented this video and saw the film when I was about 20, and this man in the white suit and his moll formed one part whose meaning I did not understand. I didn't get why they would dress up, meet in a hotel, and ask for room service. When the hotel waiter knocks on the door and enters the room, the moll is nude in bed, while the man in the white suit is fully dressed and even

理を頼んでいるのか、そういう設定がよくわかりません。ホテルマンがドアをノックして室内に入ってきたとき、情婦は裸でベッドにいるけど、白服の男は正装していて帽子もかぶっているということは、今さっきこの部屋に入ってきたということでしょう。その後、男が色んな食材を使って情婦を調理していくわけですが、僕らを引き付けるのは、あるいはついつい笑ってしまうのは情婦のヘソの上で紹興酒に閉じ込められた海老を踊らせるシーンです。全然意味がわからないですよね。

僕は大人になって、たくさんの伊丹十三の本を読み、彼がすごく食通だということを知り、紹興酒の中で海老を暴れさせるという調理法の「酔蝦（酔っ払い海老）」という広東料理があることも知りました。白服の男がこの映画の冒頭で、映画館でポテトチップスを食べる人に怒鳴るシーンがありますよね。彼にとって映画は非日常だから、下らない一般の人間の日常をはさんで欲しくないというわけです。彼にとって、映画は非日常のことなんです。彼は、伊丹十三は、非日常の映画の中でセックスをして海老を食べて死にたいんです。

大人になってからわかることってあります。僕は二十七年間バーテンダーという、真夜中にそんなに安くもないお酒を恋人たちに提供する仕事を続けてきて、大人たちがどれだけ下らない日常に辟易していて、高いお金やリスクを支払って非日常を追い求めているかということを知りました。

世の中には昼間の外が明るいときにホテルの中でしか会えない恋人たちもいるというわけです。

林 伸次（はやし・しんじ）
bar bossa 店主／小説家

レコード屋、ブラジル料理屋、バー勤務を経て、1997 年渋谷に bar bossa をオープン。選曲 CD、CD ライナー執筆、著書多数。2018 年小説家としてのデビュー作『恋はいつもなにげなく始まってなにげなく終わる。』（幻冬舎）を発表。

不倫

wearing his hat, probably meaning that he has only just come in. After that, the man places various foods on the woman's body, but what really draws us in, or makes us laugh, is the scene in which the shrimp immersed in Shaoxing wine dances on her navel. This scene makes no sense at all.

As I grew older and read a lot of Juzo Itami's books, I learned that he was very much a gourmet and that this style of cooking in which shrimp writhe in Shaoxing wine is a Cantonese dish called "zuì xiā" or "drunken shrimp." There's a scene at the beginning of the movie where the man in the white suit shouts at another man for eating potato chips in the theater. For him, a film is something extraordinary, and he does not want to be interrupted by the everyday life of someone boring and normal. To the man and Juzo Itami, a film is extraordinary. The man, and Juzo Itami, want to have sex, eat shrimp, and die in an extraordinary movie.

There is something I understood after I grew up. In my 27 years as a bartender, supplying alcohol that is not cheap late at night to lovers, I have learned the degree to which adults, bored to tears with their dull, ordinary lives, will pay for expensive alcohol and risk in pursuit of the extraordinary.

In this world, there are lovers who can only meet in hotels during the day when all outside is bright.

Translation_Ian MacDougall

Shinji Hayashi
Owner, bar bossa / Novelist

Hayashi opened his bar, bar bossa, in 1997 after working in a record store, a Brazilian restaurant, and bartending. He has curated CD anthologies, written liner notes, and authored many books. In 2018 he debuted as a novelist with *You Always Stumble into Love, You Always Stumble out of Love* (Gentosha).

Voices of Outsiders   2

Interview_Makoto Miura (COLAXO)
Photographs_Yoko Takahashi
Translation_Trivector Co., Ltd.

ずっと気になる人だった。自分は料理人だと言い切るけれど、その実態はとても多面的。キッチンを飛び出して、米シェ・パニースのシェフたちと食＆アートのイベント「OPEN harvest」を開催すれば、そこから派生して日本のシェフとも「nomadic kitchen」と冠し生産者との複合的な繋がりを構築する。大都会の東京を拠点にしつつ、土に近い視点でさまざまな"おいしい"の意味を教えてくれる彼女もきっと『タンポポ』を観たことがあるだろう。そんな思い込みだけでインタビューを申し込み、自分の予感が外れていなかったことに安堵した。

『eatrip』は料理人である野村友里がかつて監督した映画作品であり、現在経営するレストランの名前であり、彼女がずっと貫く生き方そのものを言い表している。人と食を巡り、時間と記憶を共有し、そして未来へと向かう旅。その道中幾度となく目にしたという『タンポポ』が彼女の心にどう映り、なにを語りかけていたのか。実際にラーメンを作ってもらいながら（もちろんそのあと食べながら）話を聞く幸運を得た。

I've always been curious about her. She says she is just a chef, but in reality, she's multifaceted. Stepping out of the kitchen to hold the "OPEN harvest" food and art event with chefs from Chez Panisse in the U.S., she then establishes a "nomadic kitchen" with Japanese chefs, building multidimensional connections with producers. While based in the big city of Tokyo, she teaches us the various meanings of "delicious" from a perspective close to the earth. Surely, she'd seen *Tampopo*. I asked for an interview based solely on this assumption and was relieved that my hunch was not off.

Eatrip is the name of a film that chef Nomura Yuri once directed, the name of the restaurant she now manages, and the very expression of how she has always lived. A journey through people and food, sharing time and memories, into the future. How did *Tampopo*, which she saw many times along the way, come off to her? What did it say to her? I had the good fortune of actually having her make me ramen (and eating it afterward, of course) while I listened to her stories.

野 村 友 里 (eatrip)
Yuri Nomura

『タンポポ』は食を切り口に、生と死とエロスを描く手法がほかのどの国の作品よりも際立っている

— 『タンポポ』をラーメンではなく"食"の映画として意識したのは？

自分で映画を撮るための準備をしていた頃ですね。私が監督した『eatrip』は2009年の公開だったので、2008年頃かと。構想を練る過程でさまざまな国の食にまつわる映画を探しては観ていく中で、ヨーロッパなら『バベットの晩餐会』とか、アメリカなら『ディナーラッシュ』などをピックアップしながら、日本の作品で印象的だったのが『タンポポ』と『スーパーの女』でした。どちらも伊丹十三監督作品。特に『タンポポ』は食を切り口に、生と死とエロスを描く手法がほかのどの国の作品よりも際立っていて、何度も観るようになりました。

— そもそも映画を撮ることに至ったきっかけを教えてください

当時は"ロハス"っていう言葉が流布しはじめていて、私はずっと違和感を感じていました。どこか強制的な考え方だと思っていたし、むしろこれは生き方じゃないかと感じた矢先、自分の周りにそれを実践している人たちが既にいた。彼らへのインタビューが結果的に映画という形になったのです。出演者のひとりであるシンガーのUAは大学で映画を専攻していたのでフィルムでの撮影を勧めてくれたり、彼女がちょうど妊娠したこともあり出産を待って授乳シーンを撮影しましたが、ここには『タンポポ』へのオマージュが含まれます。『タンポポ』はエンドロールに授乳の様子が差し込まれますから。

— ご自身の映画で伝えたかったことは？

今でもあの映画は作品というよりドキュメンタリーだと思っているんです。食べる行為を媒介にして、彼らの生き方を追い、誰のどの部分を切り取っても意味がある。それをどう受け止めるかは観る人に委ねました。結果として5カ国を巡って公開されたことで、食べることが生きることを意味するのであり、それが万国共通の概念なんだっていう確信を得ることができました。その手応えのような感覚は、私が働いていたサンフランシスコのオーガニックレストラン「シェ・パニース」の仲間に観てもらったときも同じようにありました。

Tampopo stood out from all others in its approach to depicting life, death and eros through the lens of food

What made you think of Tampopo as a "food" film rather than a ramen film?

It was when I was preparing to make my own film. The film, *eatrip*, was released in 2009, so I think it was around 2008. While developing the idea, I searched for and watched films related to food from various countries, picking up *Babette's Dinner* from Europe and *Dinner Rush* from the U.S. The Japanese films that impressed me were *Tampopo* and *Supermarket Woman*. Both films are directed by Juzo Itami. In particular, *Tampopo* stood out from all others in its approach to depicting life, death, and eros through the lens of food, and I have come to watch it again and again.

What led you to make a film in the first place?

At the time, the term LOHAS (lifestyles of health and sustainability) was just beginning to spread, and I always felt uncomfortable with it. I thought it was a somewhat forced way of thinking. Feeling that this was rather a way of life, I found people around me who were already practicing it. The interviews with them ended up taking the form of a film. One of the performers, the singer UA, was a film major in college and encouraged me to shoot on film. She had just become pregnant, and we waited until she gave birth to shoot the breastfeeding scene, which includes a tribute to *Tampopo*. In *Tampopo*, a scene of a woman breastfeeding is inserted in the end roll.

What did you want to convey in your film?

I still think of it as more of a documentary than a work of art. We follow their way of living through the medium of the act of eating, and any of the parts about any of the characters are meaningful on their own. We left it up to the viewer to decide how they would perceive it. As a result, the film's public release, which toured five countries, convinced us that eating means living, and this is a universal concept. That same sense of responsiveness was present when I asked my colleagues at Chez Panisse, the organic restaurant near San Francisco where I worked, to watch it.

前提としてさまざまなサイドストーリーの中ですべてにおいて
「食べる」ことが描かれていて、
どんな状況下にあってもそれが「生きる」ことに繋がっている。

— シェ・パニースで働こうと思ったきっかけは？

『eatrip』を撮ったことで図らずも自分と料理の世界との間に距離ができてしまったように感じてしまったのです。もともと言葉に長けているわけではないのに映画を撮ったからにはそれを説明していかなければいけない。原点回帰というか、また料理の世界に没頭したいと思っていた矢先、シェ・パニースの哲学に惹かれたのです。技術の追求ではなく、創業者のアリス・ウォータースが "おいしい革命" と謳った食の概念。最たるは地域における生産者・料理人・消費者が相互作用する強い横の繋がり。それらは当時の日本では体感することができないことでした。

— ちなみにシェ・パニースの関係者は『タンポポ』を知っていましたか？

知ってましたね。というのも当時のヘッドシェフで、現在は神田で「the Blind Donkey」を営むジェローム・ワーグは日本の映画通だったし、創業者であるアリス・ウォータースもゴダールのエージェントを務めるような友人がいたからから、彼らはおしなべて映画に対する造詣が深かったわけで、そもそも『タンポポ』に惹かれるような同じ感覚があったからこそウマが合ったし、現在に至る長い付き合いができているとも思います。

—『タンポポ』のサイドストーリーで印象的なシーンを教えてください

前提としてさまざまなサイドストーリーの中ですべてにおいて「食べる」ことが描かれていて、どんな状況下にあってもそれが「生きる」ことに繋がっている。そういう意味でラストの授乳シーンはやはり一番印象的ですね。母乳は人間が最初に口にするものですし、アリス（・ウォータース）も著書で語っているように、母親が口にしたものがお腹にいる子を育む。つまり食自体が未来を作り上げることを描写している。それはやはり伊丹さんが食に対して深い造詣があったからできたことではないでしょうか。

In all of the various side stories,
eating is depicted, and no matter what the situation,
they are connected with living.

What made you decide to work at Chez Panisse?

I had felt as if the filming of *eatrip* had unintentionally created a distance between me and the culinary world. I'm not a skilled wordsmith by nature, but now that I'd made a film, I had to explain it. Just as I was looking to return to my roots, or rather, immerse myself in the culinary world again, I was drawn to the philosophy of Chez Panisse. It is not a pursuit of technique but a concept of food that founder Alice Waters described as the "delicious revolution." Most important is the strong horizontal connections between producers, chefs, and consumers in the region. These were things that could not be experienced in Japan at that time.

By the way, did anyone associated with Chez Panisse know of Tampopo?

Yes, they knew about it. The head chef at the time, Jérôme Waag, who now runs the Blind Donkey in Kanda, was a Japanese movie buff. And Alice Water had a friend who was an agent for Jean-Luc Gorard, so they all had a deep knowledge of movies. I think it is because we have something like an attraction to *Tampopo* that we hit it off and have built a long relationship that continues to this day.

What scene in the side stories of Tampopo left the biggest impression on you?

In all of the various side stories, eating is depicted, and no matter what the situation, they are connected with living. In that sense, the last scene of breastfeeding is still the most impressive. Breast milk is the first thing a human being eats, and as Alice (Waters) says in her book, what a mother eats nurtures the child in her belly. In other words, that scene depicts how food itself creates the future. I think this was possible because of Itami's deep acquaintance with food.

I feel that the shared experience of eating
the same food at the same time has
an advantage over other forms of expression.

―ほかにも好きなサイドストーリーはありますか？

瀬死の母親が炒飯を作るシークエンスは、人間はいつか必ず死ぬからこそ、生きている間になにかを繋げたいという衝動のようなものを感じました。自分の母親も料理人で、目の前にお腹をへらした人が居たならば必ず満たしてあげたいという献身的な愛の持ち主。料理で職人としての技を極めるというより、家庭的なおもてなしを好んでいて、私も母がそうしている様子や空間が大好きでした。命を繋ぐことの意味を、写真や言葉で伝えることももちろんできます。でも同じ時間に、同じものを口にする "食" の共有体験には、ほかの表現よりもアドバンテージがあると感じています。

同じ時間に、同じものを口にする "食" の共有体験には、ほかの表現よりも**アドバンテージ**があると感じています。

Are there any other side stories you like?

Watching the sequence in which the dying mother makes fried rice, I felt something like the impulse that one has to connect while alive precisely because one will surely die someday. My mother is also a cook, and she possesses a self-sacrificing love that always wants to satiate anyone hungry in front of her. Rather than mastering professional cooking techniques, she preferred family-style hospitality, and I loved how my mother did so and the space she created. We can, of course, convey through pictures and words the meaning of connecting life. However, I feel that the shared experience of eating the same food at the same time has an advantage over other forms of expression.

— その考え方が、野村さんの幅広い活動に繋がるのでしょうか?

料理人であれば、おいしい料理を作ることは当然の営み。でもその"おいしい"の判断基準はさまざまで、自分がそれを競う世界で一番になりたいわけじゃない。それよりむしろ"おいしい"体験はおいしい食材によって導かれるもので、料理人はあくまでその仲介役。よく食材に料理させてもらっているように感じます。そして食材に目を向けたならば、それを育てた土のことも種のことも考えるようになるし、そこまできてやっとロハスもSDGsもはじめて身近なこととして感じられるようになる。今目の前にあるものから、その先にあるものを見つけて、どうやって未来へと繋いでいけるのかを考える。料理人の仕事が必ずしも包丁を握り続けることだけじゃない。必要があればたまには包丁を置くし、逆に仲間が必要なときは包丁を集めて場を作る。いろんな役割があっていいと思います。

How is this way of thinking connected to your wide range of activities?

If you're a chef, it's only natural to make delicious food. But the criteria for judging "delicious" vary, and I do not want to be the best in a world where I have to compete for it. Rather, the "delicious" experience is guided by delicious ingredients, and the chef is merely an intermediary. I often feel like I am being allowed to cook by the ingredients. And once you focus on the ingredients, you will start thinking about the soil and seeds that grew them, and only then will you be able to feel like LOHAS and the SDGs are near and dear. From what is in front of us now, we find what lies ahead and think about how we can connect it to the future. A cook's job is not necessarily just to continue to hold their knife. Sometimes I put down the knives if I need to, and conversely, if I need a companion, I gather the knives and create an opportunity to use them. I think it is good to have many different roles.

野村友里（のむら・ゆり）
料理人

おもてなし教室を開く、母・野村紘子さんの影響を受けて料理の道に。主な活動に、レセプションパーティーなどのケータリングフードの演出、料理教室、雑誌の連載、ラジオ番組など。2012年、東京・原宿に「restaurant eatrip」、19年、表参道・GYRE に「eatrip soil」をオープン。

Yuri Nomura
Chef

Nomura started her career in cooking, influenced by her mother, Hiroko Nomura, who holds hospitality classes. Her main activities include directing presentations of catered food for reception parties, hosting cooking classes, magazine serials, and radio programs. In 2012, she opened "restaurant eatrip" in Harajuku, Tokyo, and in 2019, "eatrip soil" in Omotesando's GYRE.
https://restaurant-eatrip.com/

THERE WAS A TIME

Photographs by Parker Fitzgerald

室町砂場（赤坂）
Muromachi Sunaba, AKASAKA

食事制限から"勝手に"解放された老人（大滝秀治）が喉を詰まらせ、隣り合わせたタンポポ（宮本信子）たちが掃除機まで駆使して死の淵から救う場面の舞台となったのは、明治二年（1869年）創業で天ざる・天もり発祥の店『室町砂場』の赤坂支店。現在も営業中。

In this soba restaurant, in business since 1869, Tampopo (Nobuko Miyamoto) uses a vacuum cleaner to save the life of an old man (Hideji Otaki) who has managed to escape his dietary minders and begins to choke on the food he is usually forbidden to eat.

エレガンス　　　Elegance

「コイツら、結構うるさくてねぇ」

「深い生活をしておるんです、コイツら」

Words of Outsiders

6

You guys are so picky!   These guys live life to the full.

自由人たちのエレガンス
——巴里の空の下オムライスのにおいは流れる——

猫沢エミ

現在のフランス人パートナーに、私が最初に見せた日本映画は、なにを隠そう『タンポポ』だった。きちんと彼に理解して欲しくて、フランス語字幕付きのDVDをわざわざネットで探して買い、パリまで持ってきて一緒に観たのだ。今ほど、まだサブスクリプションが広まっていなかった10年くらい前の話。"メディア"という"アイディアを入れる箱"だけが、ものすごいスピードでバージョンアップしていく昨今に、つい置いてけぼりになりがちな我々人間の体という柔らかな箱と、そこに宿る心。『タンポポ』を再見するたび、鮮度を失わない感動の普遍性に、人の体と心の進化は、メディアほどスピードメーターがブチ壊れてはいないのだと安堵する。

メディアといえば、稀代の粋人・伊丹十三氏は51歳という遅咲きの監督デビューに至るまで、イラストレーターや商業デザイナーなど、さまざまなメディアの世界で自己表現を重ねてきた、まさにプロの"箱の中身を作る人"。その傍ら、ひとりの人間としても実社会で重ねた多種多彩な経験値が、伊丹映画を観る際に必ず感じる、むせかえるような生の息吹(エロス)と、それを浮かび上がらせる何ものかの終わり=死(タナトス)のコントラストに色を添えている。伊丹氏がデビューした年齢と同じ51歳でふたたびパリへ舞い戻っ

The Elegance of the Free-spirited

—Under the skies of Paris, Rice Omelettes Smell good —

Emi Necozawa

The first Japanese movie I showed my present French partner was, believe it or not, *Tampopo*. Wanting him to understand it perfectly, I deliberately sought out and purchased a DVD with French subtitles on the internet and took it to Paris, where we watched it together. This was about ten years ago, before subscription services had become as popular as they are now. Today, when the "box just to put in ideas" known as "media" is being upgraded at a ferocious speed, the soft box of our human body and the heart that dwells within it tend to be left behind. Every time I see *Tampopo* again, I am reassured by an ever-present, ever-fresh

excitement that the speedometer governing the evolution of body and soul is not as broken as that of the media.

Speaking of media, before the brilliant sophisticate Juzo Itami finally bloomed with his directorial debut at the age of 51, he had found personal expression in such areas as illustration and commercial design as a professional "creating the contents of the box." Tangentially, the different levels of experience accumulating to one human being in the real world add color to the contrast one is sure to feel on seeing an Itami film, between the smothering breath of life (Eros) and the end

た私は、食やヨーロッパ文化にも造詣が深い、この稀代の粋人に、僭越ながらシンパシーを感じているのである。

　と、話は冒頭に戻るが、特に日本文化に傾倒してもいない、ごく普通のフランス人である彼が『タンポポ』を観たら、どんな感想を持つのか？　は、私にとって長年の関心事だった。と言うのも、ここまで日本人の食に対する病的なまでの欲望と、一見するところわかりにくく、しかし一皮めくれば底なしの多様性に満ちた日本のエロスを端的に見せてくれる映画は他にないからだ。映画終了後、彼がまず叫んだのは「Vous êtes fous──君ら日本人はキチ◯イだ！」であった（笑）。ヤクザと情婦が口で移し合う卵の黄身は、決して生で卵を食べないフランス人にとって、よけい見てはいけないものを見た気持ちだっただろうし、そのヤクザが流す鮮血と牡蠣の偶然の出逢いは、無論、処女の純潔と、女としての目覚めを意味しているが、こんな艶かしい手法で魅せられては返答のしようもない、というのが彼の本音だろう。

　むき身の日本人が見せる食とエロスは、生の豊かさを謳い上げる命の讃歌であり、それを浮かび上がらせる同じだけの何ものかの終わり＝死（タナトス）もまた

伊丹映画に貫かれるテーマのひとつだ。この死にも、食とエロスと同じだけの多様性がある。たとえばこの映画に登場するホームレスたちは、社会的な立場を葬り去った人々と解釈することもできる。映画が公開された1985年は、経済がバブル景気時代を迎える、まさに夜明け前。高度成長期で生まれた物質主義の価値観や〝会社の奴隷〟という表現に揶揄される仕事最優先の生き方に、早くも伊丹氏は疑問を抱いていたことになる。タンポポにスープの作り方を教えるセンセイは、妻と事務長に病院をのっとられた元産婦人科のお医者さま。彼の人間としての高い知性と品格（ただ、ちょっと世渡り下手）は、自由を獲得したホームレスたちの真の師となる。資本主義者のシステムから外れ、物質社会から逃れたホームレスたちは、想像もできないほど豊かな食生活を送り、知性溢れる探究心で日々の生活を楽しみ、そして旅立つセンセイに『仰げば尊し』を歌い贈る心の絆を持っている。その中のひとり、細身のホームレスがタンポポの息子・ターボーにオムライスを作ってあげるエピソードがいい。チャップリンやバスター・キートンを思い起こさせるコミカルな動きと音楽に乗って、真夜中の洋食屋の厨房に入り込んだふたりが、警備員の目を華麗にかわして極上のオムライスをこしらえる。知恵と人生を楽しむ心があれ

of whatever it is which brings that to the surface = death (Thanatos). For me, returning to Paris at the age of 51, the same age at which Itami made his first film, I felt a sense of both presumption and sympathy towards this brilliant sophisticate, with his depth of knowledge of both cuisine and European culture.

To return to my starting point, how would a perfectly ordinary Frenchman with no particular interest in Japanese culture react when he saw *Tampopo*? This had interested me for years. There was no other movie that would directly show to this extent the almost pathological Japanese lust for food and, although this is hard to perceive at first glance, the endless diversity of Japanese eroticism. When the movie was over, the first thing he did was shout, "Vous êtes fous/You're all crazy!" (laugh) A French person who would never eat raw eggs, seeing the yolk passed between the yakuza gangster and his mistress, would probably feel he had seen something he should never have. While the chance encounter between the blood of the gangster and the oyster suggests, of course, virginal chastity and awakening as a woman, his honest opinion would likely be that one should probably not respond to the fascination of seduction like this.

The appetite for food and Eros that the Japanese show when they come out of their shell is a hymn to life, celebrating its richness. And the end of something (= death or Thanatos) bringing to light such celebration is also a theme that pervades Itami's films. Death itself also has the same diversity as food and Eros. For example, the homeless people who appear in this film can be interpreted as those who have buried their social position. The year the film was released, 1985, was the time before the dawn as Japan approached its age of the bubble economy. The materialist values and the lifestyle of "work before all" satirized in the expression "corporate slavery" during the country's era of high economic growth are things that Itami had doubts about from an early age. The doctor who teaches Tampopo how to make broth is a former obstetrician whose wife and office manager have usurped his clinic. His wisdom as a human being and his dignity (although he lacks worldly wisdom) make him a spiritual guide for the homeless, who have attained freedom. These people, who have stepped away from the capitalist system and are fleeing from materialism, eat far better than anyone would imagine, spend their days in the pursuit of wisdom, and are tied to the doctor with bonds of the heart to the extent that they sing the traditional

ば、夢は叶うと歌うかのように。真のエレガンス——優雅とは、金や物質で形作られるものではなく、生きる志に宿る輝きそのものを指す。そして映画公開当時、日本で忘れ去られようとしていた人生のエレガンスについて、伊丹氏は自由人たちを生き生きと描き、アンチテーゼを投げかける。

物質社会からの完全離脱……とまではいかなくとも、少なくとも日本にいる時よりは、日常を送る慎ましやかな時間そのものを味わいたいとパリへ引っ越してきた私には、このエピソードがことさら沁みる。ましてやパリの空の下で再見すると、石井好子さんの『巴里の空の下オムレツのにおいは流れる』ならぬ、『巴里の空の下オムライスのにおいは流れる』……と、急に食べたくなって作った映画に登場する、あのタンポポオムライス。伊丹氏発案、日本橋『たいめいけん』の名物料理だ。まるで処女のやわ肌のごときオムレツに、禁断のナイフを一筋入れれば、その本性をあらわにした半熟卵のエロスが流れ出す。ここでも「Vous êtes fous」を繰り出した彼のいちばん好きな日本料理が、オムライスになったことは言うまでもない。

猫沢エミ（ねこざわ・えみ）
ミュージシャン／文筆家／映画解説者／生活料理人

2002～2006年、一度目のパリ在住。2007年より10年間、フランス文化誌『Bonzour Japon』の編集長を務める。超実践型フランス語教室《にゃんフラ》主宰。著書に『ねこしき』（TAC出版）、『猫と生きる。』『パリ季記』復刊版（ともに扶桑社）など多数。2022年2月より愛猫を引き連れ、二度目のパリ在住。

school graduation song *Aogebatotoshi* as he takes his leave. One episode, in which one skinny homeless man makes a rice omelette for Tampopo's son Tabo, is very good. With music and movement reminiscent of a Chaplin or Buster Keaton film, the two sneak into the kitchen of a western-style restaurant in the middle of the night, completely avoiding the eye of the night watchman to create a top-quality omelette. It is as if the song is saying that dreams do come true, given wisdom and enjoyment of life. This indicates that true elegance is not of things formed of money and materials but of the radiance in which the will to live resides. And when the film was first released, as this elegance was about to be forgotten in Japan, Itami provided an antithesis in his lively portrayal of free people.

Complete withdrawal from the materialist society...even without going that far, having moved to Paris out of a wish to experience modest everyday existence as it really is, at least to the degree that I could not do in Japan, this episode made a deep impression on me. Seeing it again under the skies of Paris, unlike chanson singer Yoshiko Ishii's essay *Sous le Ciel de Paris, ça Sent bon les Omelettes* ("Under the Skies of Paris, Omelettes Smell Good "), for me, it was "under the skies of Paris, rice omelettes smell good." What I suddenly wanted to eat, and thus made, was the *Tampopo* rice omelette. Created from Itami's own recipe, it is a specialty of the famous Taimeiken restaurant in Tokyo's Nihonbashi area. With this omelette, soft as a virgin's skin, once the forbidden knife is inserted, the Eros of that coddled egg flows forth in all its truth. There is no need to say that rice omelette is the favorite Japanese dish of that man who again shouted, "Vous êtes fous!"

Translation_Ian MacDougall

Emi Necozawa
Musician / Writer / Movie Critic / Lifestyle Chef

Emi first resided in Paris from 2002 to 2006.She was the editor of the French literature magazine *Bonzour Japon* for ten years from 2007. Emi is also the chairperson of the "super-practical" French language school Nyanfura. She has written many publications, including *Nekoshiki* (TAC Publishing), *La vie avec un chat*, and *Mon journal des quatre saisons à Paris* (both Fusosha Publishing). She returned to Paris with her pet cat in February 2022.

五色橋（海岸）
Goshiki Bashi, KAIGAN

ガン（渡辺謙）とその仲間の手によってメイクアップされたタ
ンポポ（宮本信子）は、ゴロー（山崎努）を焼肉デートへと誘
い出す。理想のロケーションを求め、当時はスナックの店内を
即席改装して焼肉店に。その窓から見えたのがこのモノレール。

Tampopo (Nobuko Miyamoto), having been made up by Gan (Ken
Watanabe) and his friends, invites Goro (Tsutomu Yamazaki) on a date
at a yakiniku grill restaurant. The search for the perfect location led to a
"Snack" bar being fitted out as the restaurant. Seen outside the window
is the Tokyo Monorail Haneda Airport Line.

オルガズム
Orgasm

Photograph_Yosuke Suzuki   Styling_Miwako Tanaka

○ ホテル【豪華なルームサービス】

卵の殻を割る音

吐息

呻き声

Words of Outsiders

In front of the hotel's opulent room-service meal.

the sound of cracking a raw egg

exhales

moans

タンポポに潜む、あなたの知らないエロス

湯山玲子

キリスト教の有名な教えの一つに、七つの大罪、というものがある。人間を罪に導く可能性がある欲望というものが7つ存在するという教えだが、その中に「貪食（どんしょく）」と「淫蕩（いんとう）」という、飲食行為とセックスが並びで掲げられている。とは言っても、このふたつは、人間が生きるために行っている日常的行為。なので、人々がそれらを続けて生きていけるように神様がそこに「快楽」というご褒美をつけてくださったことが、そもそもの間違いだったのだろうか？

その後、人間は文明を発展させ、農耕社会は備蓄という余剰を発生させることとなった。今現在、食べるという行為はグルメ・エンターテイメント化。ミシュラン星取りレストランを訪問し、インスタ栄えのする、もはや増殖した※マタンゴにしか見えないカロリー過多のパフェを食べ歩くこととなった私たちはすでに「貪食（どんしょく）」のまっただ中にいるわけだ。過＆拒食症、ダイエット、成人病なんぞはまだ自業自得だが、動植物の乱獲などによる環境破壊が地球の大問題になっている有り様なのだ。

それでも、行為自体は太古の昔と変わらないグルメはまだいい。大きく様変わりしたのは、セックスの方だ。そちらは現在、AVやそのヴァーチャル化によって実際の行為と快楽の切り離しが徹底的に行われて、ちょっと前だったら一部マニアの領域だったSMやスカトロ等のアブノーマルな快楽もギャグのネタにできるほど一般化してしまった。思えば、結婚とは思う存分セックスができる社会的装置だったわけだが、それは今ではパワーを失い、その一方で、出会い系サイトの登場で、ナンパや恋愛という面倒くさい人間関係を経由しないワンナイトスタンドはお手軽状態だ。

七つの大罪の中でも、近年際立ってその存在を発しだした食とセックスだが、インターネット登場以前の、あらゆる情報はマスコミ経由のみ、という時代には、大衆が食とセックスの欲望の渦に巻き込まれすぎることはなかった。そんな時代に、伊丹十三は限られた人々のみが体験できた、快楽的なそれらの知見をふんだんに使って、この映画を作ったのだが、時代の予見という点からは、大当たりと大外れ、両極の結果に至るところが面白い。

※「マタンゴ」…1963年に公開された日本の特撮ホラー映画。舞台となる無人島には不気味なキノコ以外に食料はまったくなく、やがてそれを食べた者はキノコ人間＝マタンゴと化していく。

The Unknown Eros Lurking in *Tampopo*

Reiko Yuyama

The Seven Deadly Sins are among most famous teachings of Christianity. They teach that there are seven desires with the potential to lead people into sin, but among these, "gluttony" and "lust," the acts of eating and drinking, and of sex, are listed together. Both are, however, everyday acts people perform to live. Was God mistaken in making these "pleasures" a reward so that humanity would continue living?

As time passed, humanity developed civilization and the ability to store agricultural surplus. Today, eating has been transformed into gourmet entertainment. We visit restaurants with Michelin stars, show it off on Instagram, and as we go around snacking on over-caloried parfaits that look like nothing so much as the mushrooms in the movie *Matango** we are probably well into "gluttony" already. Bulimia/anorexia, diets, and various adult diseases are our consequences, but we are in a state where environmental destruction due to over-consumption that could ruin the planet is becoming a serious problem.

*Matango: a 1963 Japanese science-fiction/horror movie. The only things edible on a strange desert island are mushrooms, and those who eat them eventually become "Matango"–human mushrooms.

However, we need not concern ourselves with gourmets, whose conduct remains unchanged from ancient times. The great change has come about with sex. Today, with audio-visual and virtualization separating the sexual act and the pleasure, the abnormal pleasures of sadomasochism or scatology, until recently the domain of a small number of enthusiasts, have become normal entertainment to the extent that they are the stuff of jokes. Come to think of it, while marriage was once the social mechanism allowing one to have as much sex as one desired, it has now lost its power, and in addition, the rise of online dating sites has made lightly undertaken one-night stands possible without the need for such troublesome human connections as flirting or falling in love.

While among the seven deadly sins, it is gluttony and lust that had thrust themselves forward in recent years. Before the rise of the internet, when information of various kinds came to us via mass media, the wider public had yet to be fully dragged into a maelstrom of desire for food and sex. When he made this movie, Juzo Itami was able to use an expertise with regard to food and sex that only a limited number of people had experienced, but in terms of forseeing the times, it is interesting that the results are two opposites; a solid hit and a complete miss.

大当たりはもちろんグルメ方面。ラーメンは、2000年以降海外にも進出するグローバルなメニューとなり、映画に登場するような指南役のセンセイたちは、もはや専門コンサルタントとして憧れの職業と化している。グランメゾンでビールと舌平目しか頼めない会社重役たちを尻目に、「僕は今朝からコルトン・シャルルマーニュの気分なんだ。81年はあるかしら?」とのたまう若造は、当時、非常にレアな存在だったが、今となっては、IT社長に、ソムリエ資格がある元CAなど、そんな蘊蓄を語るヤツは珍しいことではなくなったからである。

その一方で、大外れはセックス。映画中、数々のエピソードに展開していく、男と女の豊かな性愛は、その後、バブルで盛り上がったものの今ではジリ貧状態なのだ。若い世代においてのセックスはどんどん絵空事感が強くなり、それらを堪能している男女はリア充として疎まれる対象にさえなってしまっている。その代わりに、熱を帯びて追いかけ、憧れる ※「推シ」との、決して実ることのないイメージだけの性愛関係だ。もし、今この監督が生きていて、『タンポポ』の続編を撮ったとして、このセックスの現状を背景に、どんな性愛エピソードが生まれるのだろうか、と想像するにかなり絶望的な心持ちになる。

※「推シ」…自分が好きなアイドルやメンバーのことを意味する

さて、食とセックス、この二大快楽は、全ての人間にとって身近なものだけに、映画のテーマとしては王道のはずだが、これらの「快楽の本質」自体を正面切って描かれた作品はあまり多くない。なぜならば、双方共に「個人それぞれが体感する個的な快楽」だから（私のキモチイイ、はアナタのそれとは同じではないということです）。音楽を言葉で表現することが難しいように、快感や快楽は「ああ、ソレだよね！」と思わせる表現はなかなかに難しいのだ。

とはいえ、大衆の経験知がネットの登場によって、昔の王侯貴族ぐらいにレベルアップしたグルメの方は、さまざまなアプローチがなされている。食の快感をひとりメシ、というスタイルを通し、店の空間や人間関係を織り込んだ『孤独のグルメ』や、トップシェフが陥る狂気を通して、美食の魅力とそのダークサイドを描いた『ザ・シェフ』などの作品が世に出て来てもいる。

問題は、セックスの方。食べることと違って、映像だけで人々は性的快楽を引き出せるわけで、AVポルノという快楽引き出しツールが大量に流通している中

The hit was undoubtedly in the field of gourmandism. Ramen has, in the years since 2000, spread overseas to appear on the world's menus, and the various sensei who appear as instructors in the movie would today be considered specialist consultants, an occupation to which many aspire. The likes of the young employee who, under the disapproving gaze of company executives only able to order beer and meuniere at an upscale restaurant, declares that "I've felt like Corton Charlemagne all day. Would you have the '81?" could nowadays easily be seen in an IT company president or a former cabin attendant who has now qualified as a sommelier.

On the other hand, sex is a complete miss. In the movie, several episodes lead men and women into rich and rewarding sexual relations. While we saw the rise of such excitement during the bubble economy, today, the situation has deteriorated. Among the younger generation, rich sex has become a fiction, and the "normies" who enjoy relationships are being marginalized. Instead, having an "Oshi"* to chase after and admire has become a feverish compensatory act. I feel pretty hopeless when trying to imagine what sexual episodes the director would create to make Part 2 of *Tampopo* if he were alive and saw the sexual situation of today.

*Oshi: a favorite idol or member of a group.

While the two great pleasures of food and sex are profound individual experiences for us all and should serve as a classic movie theme, very few films directly portray the reality of the sensations these bring. This is because they are both pleasures each individual experiences differently. In the same way as it is difficult to find words to talk about music, it is hard to find expressions describing pleasure and its accompanying sensations that will make someone think, "Yes! That's it, isn't it!"

Having said that, the onset of the internet has brought a variety of approaches to gourmets among the common folk, whose expertise has now risen to a level once occupied only by royalty and the nobility. Through the custom of people enjoying the pleasures of food alone, various manga have appeared, such as *Kodoku no Gourmet*, which weaves together the atmosphere of restaurants and its human relations, and *The Chef*, which depicts the fascination of gastronomy and its dark side through a top chef's descent into lunacy.

Sex is a different matter. Unlike food, sexual pleasure can be invoked by images alone. It has become a serious problem today when audio-visual pornography as a tool assisting sexual pleasure is so widespread it is extremely difficult to express the

で、ツールを越えた「快楽の実像」を表現することは、至難の業なのだ。

全編ほぼセックス描写（しかも本番）というポルノスタイルにて、そこに挑んだ大島渚監督の『愛のコリーダ』。ラース・フォン・トリアー監督は『ニンフォマニアック』で色情狂の女性主人公を通し、セックスの快楽、貪欲の本質を描こうとしたが、両者とも、性的快感に潜むタナトスの方が強力に出てしまって、要すエロチックではあるが、意外にも死や破滅のイメージるに非常に深刻なものになってしまった。

そう、セックスの快楽を正面切って表現する場合、ほとんどがタナトス、つまり死と隣り合わせのそれを描くことが非常に多い。ピエル・パオロ・パゾリーニの『ソドムの市』はもちろんのこと、ミヒャエル・ハネケの『ピアニスト』、スタンリー・キューブリックの『アイズ ワイド シャット』などには常に死とダークサイドの匂いがまつわりつく。「死ぬ」というのが絶頂感の常套句なように、エクスタシーの快楽は、人間性の逸脱、意識を無化する臨死体験と隣り合わせなのだ。

しかし、『タンポポ』における、伊丹十三のアプローチは、そのタナトス方面の逆張り、つまりエロスを選択した点が際立っている。何せ、この作品の主軸は、強く感じさせてくれる。

「女の成長を見守り、助ける」というラーメンを巡るポジティブな西部劇風エンタメ・ドラマなので、そこに性を併走させて描くには、それはもう、ブレーキよりもイケイケのアクセルの方が良いに決まっているのだ。作品では本筋と並行して、パラレルにグルメのエピソードが挿入されていく。中でもグルメにちなんだ「性の快楽」は、白いスーツに身を包んだ、役所広司を主人公に展開していくのだが、それらのシーンは、をまとっていない。

まずは、白服の男とそのパートナー（彼女も白いドレスを着ている）が、ホテルの豪華なルームサービスを前に、生卵の黄身を口移しで交換するというシーン。と言ってもこのシーンの遊戯性であり、黄身交換キスを始めてしまうこの遊び心は、セックスの本番行為が黄身が崩れないように続けるこの行為は、その刺激的な体感に負けた途端、黄身がダラダラと口を汚すわけだが、それはどう考えても、射精や愛液のメタファー。

これがタナトスでなく、エロスであるゆえんは、何と言ってもこのシーンの遊戯性であり、黄身交換キスを始めてしまうこの遊び心は、セックスの本番行為が行き着くところのタナトスよりも、こそばゆいような皮膚感覚があり、生きている肉体の「愉しみ」の方を

"real image of pleasure" that transcends that tool.

A film that took on this "porno style," almost totally concerned with sex (and real sex, at that), was director Nagisa Oshima's *In the Realm of the Senses*. Lars von Trier's *Nymphomaniac*, through the erotomania of the main character, sought to portray the true nature of pleasure and lust, but in both movies, the Thanatos death instinct latent in the sexual desire came out stronger, and in the end, these were very darkly serious works.

Indeed, the vast majority of films directly expressing the pleasures of sex portray its close connection to Thanatos. The smell of death and the dark side pervades such films as, of course, Pier Paolo Pasolini's *Salo, or the 120 Days of Sodom*, but also Michael Haneke's *The Piano Teacher* or Stanley Kubrick's *Eyes Wide Shut*. In the sense that "I'm dying!" is a cliché denoting orgasm, the pleasure of ecstasy aligns with the near-death experience of departure from one's humanity and the nullification of consciousness.

However, Juzo Itami's approach in *Tampopo* is notable for its choice of Eros in contrast to Thanatos. It is, after all, a positive western-style entertainment revolving around ramen whose axis is "watching over and assisting in a woman's personal growth," so portraying sex in parallel with this, of course, requires stepping on the accelerator more than the brake. Side by side with the main story, the gourmet episodes are inserted in parallel. Among them, the gourmet-inspired "sexual pleasures" story, featuring Koji Yakusho in a white suit, is erotic but surprisingly free of images of death and destruction.

First is the scene in which the man and his partner (she is also wearing a white dress) pass a raw egg yolk from mouth to mouth in front of the hotel's opulent room-service meal. This action is performed so as not to break the yolk, but when the stimulation becomes too much, it dribbles down and stains the mouth. However you may see it, this is a metaphor for ejaculation and sperm.

What suggests more than anything that this scene is Eros rather than Thanatos is its playfulness. The yolk-swapping kiss is more about the pleasure of being alive than the spirit of Thanatos we reach with the full act of sex.

It is erotic, innocent, cheerful, and silly. It is a feeling that strongly reinforces the life affirmation of the film's main story, the ramen western. To begin with, the egg has been a symbol of vitality

エロいのだが、無邪気で明るい、そしてバカバカしい。この感覚は、映画のメインストーリーであるラーメン・ウェスタンが持つ人生肯定感を補強してあまりある。そもそも、卵というものは、古来より生命力の表徴。ちなみに、ストリップには、女性器から卵を出し入れする花電車というパフォーマンスも存在するわけで、これもまた、ある意味、手品のようにあっけらかんとプレイフルな痴戯だ。

もうひとつは、白い服の男が浜辺で、少女の海女に出逢い、彼女が捕った牡蠣を食べるというシーン。瀬戸内海のクロアワビ by 岩井志麻子でお馴染みのように、貝類、牡蠣は女性器の象徴。男はそれを少女の手から食べ、なおかつその牡蠣には、殻でうっかり唇を切った男の血が一滴たらされる。少女、破瓜（はか）の血、クンニリングスとこの一連がエロス記号満載なのは明らかだが、場面のラストには、男の唇の血を、少女が淡いキスのように、べろりと舐める極めつけにエロい場面が待ち構えている。

三島由紀夫の小説『潮騒』には、海女の少女と漁夫の少年との『ダフニスとクロエ』のような神話的なエロスが描かれたが、この牡蠣のシーンがその境地を目指したのは明らか。少女とよそ者男の性的接触は、未成年とのイケないコトであり、一般的にはアンモラルなのだが、そんな彼らの姿を海の中から、おおらかに笑って見守る海女たちの1シーンを挿入することで、セックスの快楽は、やはり陽性のエネルギーと肯定感に包まれるのだ。

ちなみに、このシーンに流れるのは、マーラーの交響曲第5番の第4楽章「アダージェット」。ヴィスコンティの映画『ベニスに死す』で、波光がきらめく中、彼方を指差す片想いの美少年を見ながら死んでいく主人公の初老男のバックに流れる曲と同様なのだが、初老男の視線の先には、輝かしい生のただ中にある少年がいるわけで、この生命の光に対する肯定感は、やはり、本作の牡蠣のシーンとシンクロしていることも興味深い。

こういった、音楽の知見、センスについても、伊丹十三監督はぬかりがない。ちなみに、性の快楽を描いたこの二つのエピソードの強度は異様に強く、観終わった後は、主軸のラーメン店繁盛記よりも、そちらの印象の方が断然強いという、逆転現象が起こってしまうのが面白いところだ。

そのほか、愛人の腹の上でエビを踊らせたり、生クリームをつけた乳房にかぶりついたりのエロエピソードがこの『タンポポ』には満載なのだが、スーパーマー

since ancient times. Incidentally, in strip shows, there is a performance called *Hanadensha* (flower train), in which an egg is inserted and removed from a woman's genitalia. This is similarly playful and nonchalant, in a sense, like a magic trick.

Another example is the scene in which the man meets a girl diver at the seaside, and eats an oyster she has caught. In the same way that the porn actress/author Shimako Iwai styles herself "the black abalone from the Inland Sea," oysters and other shellfish symbolize the female sex organs. The man eats from the girl's hand, and the oyster shell cuts his lip, which sheds a drop of blood. It is obvious this invocation of girl, pubescence, and cunnilingus is packed with erotic suggestion, but awaiting us at the end of the sequence is a more explicit scene in which the girl licks the blood directly from the man's lip as if with a light kiss.

Yukio Mishima's novel *The Sound of Waves* depicts a mythical *Daphnis and Chloe*-like eroticism between its young girl diver and young fisherman, and it is clear that this oyster scene aims for the same territory. The sexual connection between the girl and this stranger would generally be considered immoral, but the insertion of one shot of a group of older women divers watching with broad-minded smiles from in the water enwraps the pleasure of sex in positive energy and a sense of affirmation.

Also, through this scene plays the 4th Adagietto movement of Mahler's 5th Symphony. This is similar to Visconti's film *Death in Venice*, where the piece plays behind the dying elderly protagonist watching, amidst waves sparkling in the sun, the beautiful young boy he loves pointing into the distance. In the protagonist's gaze, the boy is in the midst of life in all its glory, and the sense of affirmation concerning this light of life synchronizes with the oyster scene in *Tampopo*.

Juzo Itami is thus sure-sighted in his knowledge and sense of music as well. Interestingly, the weird intensity of these two episodes portraying sex demonstrate a reversal phenomenon in that they leave a stronger impression on people than the main story of a ramen restaurant coming to prosperity.

There are other erotic scenes, such as the shrimp dancing on the belly of the gangster's lover or him licking fresh cream from one of her breasts, but one other scene that leaves an impression occurs in a grocery store, in the conflict between the proprietor and an elderly lady vandalizing such soft foods as camembert cheese and peaches by sticking her finger into them and leaving marks.

ケットで、カマンベールチーズや桃といった柔らかい食べ物に指を押しつけてへこませるという、トンデモ行為を行う老婆と店主の攻防戦も忘れてはならない。

非常にスラップスティックなシーンなのだが、触ることで、そのモノを貶めていくという行為はまさに痴漢というハラスメントそのもの。カマンベールも桃も、ネットリ、ジューシーという独特の食感を伴っているだけに、そのコミカルさの中に、エロセンスが入ってくるところが心憎い。

ところでこの作品、濃厚なエロスを含んだエピソードに対して、メインの恋愛物語はプラトニック、というような印象があったのだが、今回、改めて観て、それが間違いだったことが分かった。女主人公のタンポポは、自分に手を出してこないゴローに業を煮やし、ドレスアップして焼き肉デートに行き、その後、家にゴローを招き入れ、風呂に入らせて、どうやらその後コトに及んだような形跡があるのだ。

タンポポは色っぽい寝間着の浴衣姿で、風呂場の脱衣所の籠に脱ぎ捨ててあったゴローの汚れたパンツを、死んだ夫が箪笥に残していた未使用のブリーフと取り替える。その後に、カメラは家の外から、部屋の灯りが消えるところを一瞬映すわけだが、これらの映像言語は、「ふたりが結ばれた」と考えるのがごく自然だろう。

普通の男と女ならば、これ以降ぐっと距離は縮まるはずなのだが、伊丹十三はあえて、そのリアリティーをすっ飛ばす。ゴローはトラックの運転手稼業から足を洗って、タンポポのパートナーになり、ラーメン屋の亭主になるのが定石だろうに、ゴローはタンポポを自立させ、プロにするというミッションを優先させるのだ。ゴローにとってのタンポポは、一度セックスはしたにせよ、相変わらず、最後まで、不可侵の聖母マリアのような存在で、また、タンポポの方もその距離を縮めないのである。

本作に潜む最大エロスはここのところで、ふたりに許されたのはただ、ひと晩だけの肉体関係。映画『タンポポ』は、「相思相愛のふたりに許された最初で最後のセックス」に勝る快楽はないという話なのでありました。

湯山玲子（ゆやま・れいこ）
著述家／プロデューサー／おしゃべりカルチャーモンスター

著作に『女ひとり寿司』『女装する女』『四十路越え！』等。テレビコメンテーターとしても活躍。クラシック音楽の新しい聴き方を提案する〈爆クラ〉主宰。ファッションブランド〈OJOU〉のデザイナー・プロデューサーとしても活動している。日大芸術学部文藝学科講師。

This is an extremely slapstick scene, but degrading these items by touching them is equivalent to the groping of a molester. It is stunning how the presence of the unique sticky, juicy texture of camembert and peaches in this comedic sequence gives way to a feeling of eroticism.

Incidentally, my first impression upon seeing this film was that the central story was of platonic love, while the episodes were richly erotic, but upon seeing it again, I realized I was mistaken. The central female character Tampopo loses patience with Goro, who makes no move toward her, so she dresses up, and they go for Korean barbecue. Later she invites Goro into her house, lets him take a bath, after which what happens is only hinted at.

Wearing a sexy yukata sleeping gown, in the changing area outside the bath Tampopo exchanges the underpants Goro has left in the clothes basket, replacing it out of a chest of drawers with a new pair her late husband had evidently never worn. Following this, the camera is outside on the street when the room light goes off. It is completely natural to assume that this is movie language for "the two have joined together."

With an ordinary man and woman, after this, they would be much closer, but Juzo Itami intentionally skips over this version of reality. While Goro could be expected to abandon truck driving and become Tampopo's partner and the master of the ramen establishment, Itami gives priority to his mission of making Tampopo an independent professional. While they have slept together once, in Goro's eyes, Tampopo is a constant Holy Mother Mary-like figure to the end, while for her part, she does not close the distance between them.

This is the most erotic aspect of the film; all these two are permitted is one night of physical connection. In the film *Tampopo*, there is no greater pleasure than when "the first sex allowed between two true lovers is also the last."

Translation_Ian MacDougall

Reiko Yuyama
Writer / Producer / Talk Culture Monster

Yuyama is an author whose publications include *Lone Woman Sushi, Woman Dressed as Woman*, and *Over 40!* Also active as a television commentator. Has supervised Bakunon Classics, a new approach to listening to classical music. She also designs and produces her own fashion label, "OJOU." Lecturer in Literary Arts at Nihon University College of Art.

浜崎橋（海岸）
Hamazaki Bashi, KAIGAN

焼肉デートを終えたゴロー（山崎努）とタンポポ（宮本信子）は、
雨に打たれながらこの橋でタクシーを捕まえようとする。この
雨が図らずも二人の距離を近づける要因となることは、本書の
湯山玲子氏のコラムにて解説されている。

In the rain after their yakiniku date, Goro (Tsutomu Yamazaki) and
Tampopo (Nobuko Miyamoto) try to hail a taxi on this bridge. The scene,
which brings the two unintentionally into close contact, is the subject of
commentary by Reiko Yuyama in this volume.

How

アメリカ人の心に、ようやくタンポポが咲いた

ウィリー・ブラックモア

1980 年代、アメリカで最も手軽に食べられるラーメンといえばインスタントラーメンだった。その頃アメリカの中西部で育った私は、ヒッピー系のスーパーで両親が買ったちょっと高級なインスタントラーメンに、母お手製の豆腐と蒸したブロッコリーを加えたり、粉末調味料を入れたお湯で茹でるような、間違ったやり方で作ったチキンラーメンを友達の家で食べたことを覚えている。ロサンゼルスなど日本人が多く住む大都市では、ラーメン屋よりも寿司屋の方が庶民の間で流行っていたし、実際 1980 年代のロサンゼルス・タイムズ紙でラーメンといえば、ほとんどがインスタントラーメンの広告だった。それが 1987 年アメリカで『タンポポ』が公開されたことにより、ラーメンの認識は変わった。伊丹十三はあらゆる点において、アメリカにはじめて本物のラーメンを紹介した功労者だ。しかしアメリカ人がこの映画を本当の意味で理解できるようになったのは公開からさらに数十年後、ラーメン文化が浸透してからのことである。

Figured Out

America

Finally

In the 1980s, the most readily available type of ramen in the United States was the instant variety. As a young kid growing up in the midwest in the late '80s, I remember having the slightly fancier kind of instant ramen that came from the hippie grocery store my parents shopped at, which my mom always added bits of tofu and steamed broccoli too (we were vegetarian), and the illicit chicken Top Ramen I would eat at my friend's house, who liked to eat the noodles dry after steeping them in the seasoning packet-doused hot water. Even in major cities like Los Angeles, with its long-standing Japanese population, sushi bars were far more in vogue with the general dining public than ramen shops; in fact, most mentions of ramen in the Los Angeles Times throughout much of the 1980s are found in advertisements for instant noodles. That all changed when *Tampopo* premiered in the United States in 1987. For all intents and purposes, Juzo Itami is responsible for introducing real ramen to American audiences for the first time. And it wasn't until decades later, after Americans became more steeped in ramen culture, that they were truly able to understand the film.

Willy Blackmore

TAMPOPO

How

America   Finally

1988年にロサンゼルス・タイムズ紙に掲載されたラーメン店の批評を振り返ると、その冒頭には当時テレビで繰り広げられていたインスタントラーメンの広告合戦の様子が描かれている。「今となってはラーメン愛好家たちが、ラーメンがいわゆるインスタントラーメン（プラスチックの容器に入った乾麺）以上のものであるということを知っている」と、著者のリンダ・バラムは記している。私たちのラーメンに対する意識は外国映画愛好家の間で大ヒットした日本映画『タンポポ』によって高まったのだ。1980年代後半にこの映画にちなんだレストランがロサンゼルスで人気を博し、その後小規模チェーンが生まれ街中に支店ができたため、『タンポポ』は一時期ロサンゼルスでラーメンの代名詞にもなっていた。

1987年に公開されたこの映画の批評では、「ラーメン」という言葉がほとんど出てこないのは、つまり『タンポポ』とともに「ラーメン」がアメリカに上陸したことを物語っている。ニューヨーク・タイムズ紙の批評家ヴィンセント・キャンビーは、この映画について「少なくとも、明確な意識を持って袋麺（インスタントラーメン）を買う人を除けば一貫して面白くない」と書いている。シカゴ・トリビューン紙のロバート・エバートは、より鋭い批評で「アメリカの観客は、日本人の麺に対する熱心な探究についてほとんど知らないし関心もないように思える。しかしこの映画は非常に詳細で、『麺の美学』に完全に没頭している点において、それ自体が一種の独特な論理を持つようになった」とも書いている。とはいえロバートよ、あなたはそれが一体どんな日本の麺なのか知っていただろうか？　ましてやシカゴ・リーダー紙の批評では、ラーメンの名前は出てくるがすぐに次のような定義付けがされている：「中華麺＝日本の流行するファーストフードで、アメリカにおけるピザのようなもの」とも。

Consider a ramen shop review published by the Los Angeles Times in 1988, which opens with a description of the instant ramen ad wars that were playing out on television at the time. "By now, however, Western ramen enthusiasts know that there's much more to ramen than dehydrated noodles in a foam plastic cup," the author, Linda Burum, wrote. "Our ramen consciousness was raised by 'Tampopo,' the Japanese film that achieved blockbuster status with foreign-film aficionados." Tampopo was even synonymous with ramen in Los Angeles for a time, after a restaurant named for the movie became a destination in the late 1980s, and then later spawned a mini chain with outposts across the city in the following years.

That ramen essentially arrived in America with Tampopo helps explain the reviews of the film published in 1987, which avoid mention of the word "ramen" almost to a fault. In his review for the New York Times, critic Vincent Canby wrote that movie was "not consistently funny (at least not to someone who, with a clear conscience, buys his noodles in plastic bags)." The Chicago Tribune's Robert Ebert was more searching in his review, writing, "It might seem that American audiences would know little and care less about the search for the perfect Japanese noodle, but because the movie is so consumed and detailed, so completely submerged in noodleology, it takes on a kind of weird logic of its own." Yes, but what kind of Japanese noodle, Robert Ebert? A review from the Chicago Reader does refer to ramen by name, and quickly offers the following definition in a parenthetical: "Chinese noodles—a Japanese fast-food craze roughly akin to pizza in the U.S."

Figured Out

『タ ンポポ』の初期の批評は、食と性の関わりか、伊丹監督のマカロニ・ウェスタンの比喩に対する風刺的な扱いに帰結するばかりで、この映画の中心となる料理本来の意図を掴みかねていた。また、この映画で提示されている食べ物やセックスなど、あらゆる快楽を求め手に入れることは、人間を突き動かすのみならず、社会経済的な地位にも関係なく、生まれもっての権利であるという概念に関し、初期のレビューではほとんど触れられていない(私も『タンポポ』を何度も観るうちに、この映画のことをよく理解できるようになった。そして何度も観れば観るほど、それ＝ "快楽を手にする生まれもっての権利" がこの作品の核心であると確信する)。さらには『タンポポ』におけるサイドストーリーまでもが行き当たりばったりなものに思われていたゆえ、批評家達は読者に納得してもらうために、ありきたりな日本文化の決まり文句を持ち出した。例えばキャンビーはタイムズ紙の批評で、「これらのサイドストーリーは、タンポポと彼女の麺の教育にはあまり関係ないかもしれない」とまで書いている。「しかし、それらはすべて、食べ物や麺をすすり、花を生け、お茶を飲み、自殺することを美化してきた日本人の儀式好きと関係がある」とも。

30 年後、『タンポポ』がアメリカの映画館で再び公開され、クライテリオン・コレクションの一部として DVD 化されたとき、批評家の反応に、ラーメンへの距離感はもうなかった。『タンポポ』以降、アメリカの主要都市にラー

W ithout any real context for the film's central dish, the early *Tampopo* reviews are left grasping at meaning, most often landing on something about the connection between food and sex, or Itami's satiric treatment of Spaghetti Western tropes. There's little in these initial reviews about how Itami addresses class in *Tampopo*, with its expansive cast of blue-collar (at best) epicureans, or the notion presented in the film that desiring and attaining all things pleasurable – food and sex, sure, but so much more too – not only drives humanity but is our innate right, no matter our socioeconomic status. (The more times I watch *Tampopo*, the more I'm convinced that this is its central tenet.) Instead, *Tampopo*'s narrative side quests are seen more as random than anything else, with some critics turning to cliches about Japanese culture in order to make it all click for readers. The secondary mini and micro plots "may not have much bearing on Tampopo and her noodle education," Canby wrote in his Times review, "but they all have to do with food and with the Japanese love of ritual that has made an art of slurping noodles, arranging flowers, drinking tea and committing suicide."

T hirty years later, when a restored print of *Tampopo* was rereleased in U.S. theaters and on DVD as part of the Criterion Collection, the critical response did not shy away from ramen. After the post-*Tampopo* burst of ramen bars in major

メン屋は出現し、2010 年代には入手困難な料理から、ごく当たり前のものになった（それでもまだ驚くレベルのラーメンを見つけるのは難しい）。すでに醤油味のラーメンも豚骨味のラーメンも知るアメリカの観客が観た『タンポポ』は、まったく異なる映画として彼らの眼に映り、それは 2017 年公開のレビューにも見てとれる。「この映画は、次から次へと異なるサイドストーリーへと流れ、ヒロインの成長を確認するためにたびたび立ち止まりながら、料理は社会的地位を反映するものであり、その境界を取り払うものでもある」と、ジャスティン・チャンはロサンゼルス・タイムズ紙で評している。その批評では、ラーメンの名前が出てくるのみならず『タンポポ』が上映された劇場がリトル大阪として知られる地域の中心であるソーテル・ブルバードから車ですぐのところにあり、そこではさまざまな種類のラーメンが食べられることまで教えてくれる。

他のレビュアーも同様に、2017 年にはもうかつての点と点を、線で結べるようになっていた。『タンポポ』が食べ物とセックスについての風変わりな映画として捉えられることはなくなり、その代わりにヴィレッジ・ボイス紙が「この作品で食べ物はただ消費されるだけではなく、一口一口が人生の讃歌のようである」と伝え、ロサンゼルス・タイムズ紙では「食べ物を真剣に扱うだけでなく、あらゆる文化において食べ物が果たす基本的な役割を把握している」とも述べている。

American cities, in the 2010s ramen went from being a hard-to-find dish to something approaching commonplace (though finding transcendent ramen can still be a challenge). Watched by an audience who knows its tonkotsu from its shoyu, *Tampopo* looks like a very different film, and that's reflected in the reviews of the 2017 release. "As the movie drifts from one anecdote to another, pausing every so often to check in on its heroine's progress, it shows how cuisine is both the great social leveler and a significant delineator of class," Justin Chang wrote in the Los Angeles Times. Not only is ramen referred to by name, the review even notes that the theater *Tampopo* played at was a short drive from Sawtelle Boulevard – the heart of an area known as Little Osaka – where you can have your pick of ramen styles.

Other reviewers were similarly able to connect the dots in 2017. Gone is the narrow framing of *Tampopo* as a quirky movie about food and sex, replaced with the likes of The Village Voice declaring, "food isn't just consumed in *Tampopo* – every bite is an ode to life," and in the Los Angeles Times, "*Tampopo*" doesn't just take food seriously; it grasps the foundational roles that food plays in every culture."

私がこの前改めて『タンポポ』を観直したときに、今まであまり心に響くことがなかった、ある瞬間が目に飛び込んできた。それは、タンポポとゴローが他の様々なラーメン屋を偵察する中、あるラーメン屋でほとんど手をつけなかったのを店主に見つかってしまう場面。豚骨に火が通りすぎている、昆布が濃すぎる、アンチョビの臭いがする…など、食べられなかった理由を細かく店主に伝えると、その店主が「お前ら素人にうちのラーメンがわかるのか！」と怒鳴りつける。そしてタンポポは「おじさん、ラーメンを食べる人はみんな素人よ」と笑顔で言い返す。伊丹監督が映画の中で何度も教えてくれたように、素人だからと言ってラーメンを美味しく食べられないということはなく、ヘドニズム（快楽主義）は生まれもってのものであり、育まれるものではないのだ。

そういう意味で、『タンポポ』が公開された40年近く前のアメリカ人は、混雑したラーメン屋で麺をすする日本人と同じように素人だった。しかし、『タンポポ』は私たちに新しく、素晴らしく美味しいものを与えてくれた。以来私たちは、どうにも麺をすするのを止めることができないのだ。

There's a moment in the movie that jumped out when I last rewatched it, one that never really resonated with me before. It's during the stretch when Tampopo and Goro are spying on other ramen shops, and after they barely touch their bowls at one nearby ramen bar, they are found out by the staff. After the pair tell the owners, in detail, why they didn't eat the ramen – the pork bones were over cooked, the kombu is too heavy, and it all stinks of anchovies – one of the chefs yells, "As if you amateurs could appreciate our ramen!" Tampopo smiles, and says back, "Pops, people who eat ramen are all amateurs." And just as Itami shows us time and time again in his movie, that by no means precludes them from appreciating a perfect bowl of ramen. Hedonism is nature, not nurture.

In that sense, Americans were just like any Japanese diner slurping noodles at a crowded ramen bar when *Tampopo* was first released nearly 40 years ago: amateurs. *Tampopo* gave us a first taste of something new and wonderful and delicious, and we haven't stopped slurping since.

日本語訳_野々村万穂

ウィリー・ブラックモア
ライター／エディター

食や文化、環境を専門に扱うフリーランスのライター、エディター。ニューヨーク・タイムズ紙やロサンゼル・スタイムズ紙、Eater 等で記事を発表。ブルックリン在住。

Willy Blackmore
Writer / Editor

He covers food, culture, and the environment. His stories have been published by New York, The New York Times Magazine, The Los Angeles Times, Eater, and elsewhere. He lives in Brooklyn.

TAMPOPO

Soundtrack for Tampopo
by Kunihiko Murai

伊丹十三監督映画『タンポポ』のために村井邦彦が集めた古今東西の名曲集

STEREO WPF-60065

SIDE I

1. 交響詩『前奏曲』
Symphonic Poem "Les Préludes"
(作曲 / リスト)
小泉ひろし指揮 東京シティ・フィルハーモニック管弦楽団

2. セリフ
Dialogues

3. 楽しいオムライス作り
Fun Making Omelets
(作曲・編曲 / 安西史孝)
安西史孝・向谷 実

4. 『ファゴットとチェロのためのソナタ・変ロ長調』より
第3楽章・ロンド
Sonata for Bassoon and Cello in B-flat major, K. 292: III. Rondo
(作曲 / モーツァルト)
チェロ / 木越 洋 ファゴット / 前田信吉

SIDE II

1. DEAR MOTHER ～母の胸で見る夢は～
(原曲 /『子供のアルバム』より「辻音楽師」) 安西史孝

2. 『新ウィーン・レントラー』より
From "New Viennese Ländler"
(作曲 / ランナー) 多田ストリングス

3. 北京ダックのテーマ
Theme for Peking Duck
(作曲・編曲 / 向谷 実) 向谷 実

4. ラクエン / RAKUEN
(作曲・編曲 / 本多俊之) 本多俊之

5. 交響曲第5番 嬰ハ短調・第4楽章『アダージェット』より
Symphony No. 5 in C-Sharp Minor - IV. Adagietto
(作曲 / マーラー) 小泉ひろし指揮 東京シティ・フィルハーモニック管弦楽団

6. 愛のテーマ ～タンポポ MY LOVE ～
Love Theme –TAMPOPO MY LOVE–
(作曲 / 村井邦彦・向井 実 編曲 / 向谷 実) 向谷 実 (バイオリン / 安西一陽)

120　© ユニバーサル ミュージック

ある音楽家のサイド・ストーリー

A Composer's Side Story

この映画は、まるで私の魂を映し出しているかのような映画だと思います。私は食べ物が大好きだし、不条理も大好きです。甘美でありながら、おぞましくもある。そんな映画ですね。ときにセクシュアリティも。

ひとつ面白い話が。私たちの親友の一人であるヒロ・ムライは、ミュージックビデオの監督で、ドラマ『アトランタ』などでも活躍しています。彼はすごいんです。そして彼の父親も作曲家であり、『タンポポ』の冒頭にも登場していたのです。彼はポテトチップスをやかましく食べていて、ヤクザに殴られる男の役。

本当に素晴らしい映画ですよね。

This is a movie that like, I feel like is very much like a reflection of my soul. I love food. I love absurdity. I love, yeah, I love the way that it's like, really sweet and also really horrific. Sometimes the sexuality.

And the one fun fact one of our good friends, Hiro Murai, who is music video director who now he did it, Atlanta and stuff like that. He's incredible. His father was the composer and he was also at the beginning of the movie. He's the guy who's eating chips really loudly and gets beat up by the Yakuza.

Yeah, it's amazing.

ダニエル・クアン

（映画『エブリシング・エブリウェア・オール・アット・ワンス』の監督ダニエルズ）

Daniel Kwan
Movie director duo Daniels is known for *Everything Everywhere All at Once*

Voices of Outsiders

3

新型コロナウィルス感染症により史上はじめて1年の延期を経て開催された東京2020オリンピック・パラリンピック競技大会。その開閉会式の音楽監督をプロデューサーで選曲家の田中知之が務めたことは、ある意味東京という都市の様相を象徴する出来事だったのではないだろうか。文化的な側面において東洋に位置しながら西洋の文化を適材適所に取り込んで独自の発展を遂げた日本の首都の歴史は、編集とリミックスの痕跡を類い稀な濃さで遺しており、元編集者で現役の世界的DJが二度目となる歴史的祭典の音楽演出を請け負ったことが、今となってはとても自然だったように思える。

おまけに彼は食通だ。せんべろにカテゴライズされるB級のもつ焼き屋にも、一晩10万円もするA級モダンキュイジーヌにも等しく愛を注ぐ様は、エサ箱から拾った駄盤と世界有数のレア盤を縦横無尽にミックスするいつものあのDJプレイとなんら変わらない。だから彼からも『タンポポ』の話を聞いてみたいと思った。あの映画に収められたバラバラのショートストーリーが伊丹十三の手によって見事にミックスされたように、FPM流の奇想天外な手法で食と音の話を料理してくれる気がしたから。

期待を裏切らなかったその妙技は、創業60年を超える中華の名店「南国酒家」でお披露目された。

Due to COVID-19, the Tokyo 2020 Olympic and Paralympic Games were held after being postponed for a year, a historical first. The fact that producer and DJ Tomoyuki Tanaka served as musical director for the opening and closing ceremonies was, in a sense, symbolic of the event's aspect of Tokyo the city. The history of this capital city, which is located in the far east but has developed independently by incorporating western culture selectively and effectively, bears the imprint of editing and remixing to an exceptional degree. Looking back, it seems very natural that a former editor and today world-famous DJ was contracted to direct the music for Tokyo's second Olympics.

On top of that, he's a foodie. He pours his love equally into B-class grilled offal restaurants, known for getting you drunk for less than ten bucks, and A-class modern cuisine that costs nearly one thousand dollars a night. It's no different from his usual DJ playlist that endlessly mixes shoddy records picked out of a bin with some of the world's rarest vinyl. So, I wanted to hear about *Tampopo* from him as well. I had a feeling that he would cook up a conversation about food and sound in an unexpected FPM style, just as the disparate short stories in that film were mixed together beautifully by Juzo Itami.

He unveiled this virtuosity, which did not disappoint expectations, at the famous Chinese restaurant "Nangokushuka", which has been in business for over 60 years.

Interview_Makoto Miura (COLAXO)
Photographs_Shota Matsumoto
Translation_Trivector Co., Ltd.

田 中 知 之 (FPM)

Tomoyuki
Tanaka

Yeah, my dad loved *Tampopo.*

そう、『タンポポ』はうちの父親がすごく好きな映画でした。

— 出身である京都は、有名な中華料理店が多いですよね？

日本全国で展開していて誰もが知っている餃子の王将も天下一品も、京都が発祥ですから
ね。天下一品に関しては、南区にあるお店の方が本店より美味いとか、高校生の頃から食
べ比べて、グルメの原体験をした思い出深い場所です。あと京都と言えば真っ黒なスープ
とたっぷりの九条ネギで有名な新福菜館。とりわけ三条店がラーメンマニアにも知られる
頑固な昭和気質のお店で、うちの父親がよく連れていってくれました。腎臓が悪くて人工
透析までしていたのにラーメン屋に行くなんて命懸けの行為なんですけど(笑)。そう、『タ
ンポポ』はうちの父親がすごく好きな映画でした。

— 東京でも好きなラーメン店を挙げることができますか？

恵比寿にラーメン山田というお店があったんです。東京には珍しく札幌ラーメンのお店な
のに、僕が好きなのは味噌ではなく塩や醤油。自分のスタジオに至近のラーメン店だから
よく行ってたし、いつでも食べられると思っていたのに、ある日突然閉店してしまって。
貼り紙にはご主人が他界された旨が書かれていて、ノスタルジーを超越した絶望感に襲わ
れました。ちょうどジョエル・ロブションも同じタイミングで亡くなられましたけど、彼
はレシピもたくさん遺しているし、お弟子さんもたくさんいるからまだロブションの味は
この世に現存している。かたや親父さんひとりでやっていたラーメン山田の味は、再現が
不可能。実家のおふくろの味と一緒ですよ。だから味そのものの数値化・データ化には長
年興味があります。だってどんな優秀な AI にも実現できないことだと思いますから。

Your hometown Kyoto has many famous Chinese restaurants, no?

Gyoza no Ohsho and Tenka Ippin, both well-known throughout Japan, originated in Kyoto. The latter's where I had my formative gourmet experience, and it holds a special place in my heart. From my high school days, I'd compare the food at its different locations—noting, for example, that the branch in the Minami Ward is better than the main restaurant, and so on. And speaking of Kyoto, Shinpuku Saikan can't be left out, either. It's famous for its black soup and generous helpings of Kujo green onions. The Sanjo branch is particularly known among ramen enthusiasts for its stubborn old-fashioned Showa-era sensibility. My father used to take me there often. He had kidney problems, even going on dialysis, so going to a ramen shop was life-threatening (laugh). Yeah, my dad loved *Tampopo*.

Can you name your favorite ramen shop in Tokyo?

There was a place called Ramen Yamada in Ebisu. Even though this was Tokyo, their claim to fame was Sapporo ramen, and I liked their salt and soy sauce rather than the more common miso. I used to go there often because it was the closest ramen shop to my studio, and it was the kind of place I thought I go to anytime, but one day it suddenly closed. A notice on the door said that the owner had passed away. I was struck with despair that went beyond nostalgia. Joël Robuchon passed away around the same time, but he left behind many recipes and had many disciples, so the Robuchon taste still exists in this world. But the taste of Ramen Yamada, which was run by just this one older guy, is impossible to reproduce. It's just like mom's cooking at home. That's why I've been interested in quantifying taste and turning it into data for many years. I don't think even the best AI can do so.

それは伊丹さんも『タンポポ』の中で表現されていた

エロティシズムじゃないでしょうか。

— 美味しさにまつわる記憶もまた、数値で表すことができません

だからこそタンポポたちは理想の味を求めて映画の中でも奔走しているわけですが、実は
ひとりだけ味覚に関して共感覚を持つ人を知っています。どんな味も記憶だけを頼りにそ
の知られざるレシピに辿り着くことができる方でした。音楽で言えば絶対音感のようなこ
とかと。ただ音楽と異なることは、食べる行為って所有することができない。食べるその
瞬間を、五感を駆使して楽しむしかない。絶対に AI が辿り着けない境地であるからこそ
嫉妬するし、自分はなぜ食の道に進まなかったのかよく後悔します。

— 食の営みに勝る快楽があるとすれば、なんでしょう?

それは伊丹さんも『タンポポ』の中で表現されていたエロティシズムじゃないでしょうか。
人間の三大欲についてはたまに考えますが、うちの犬はどんなに眠たそうにしていても僕
がスナック菓子の袋を開けるとすごい勢いで走ってくるので、彼の場合食欲が睡眠欲に勝
るっていうことはよく分かっています(笑)。僕自身エロティシズムをテーマに音楽を作
ることが多々ありますし、音楽のみならずあらゆるエンタメの根底に通奏低音として流れ
ている。人間のクリエイティビティーを刺激する、大切な概念だと思っています。

—『タンポポ』におけるエロティシズムで印象深かったのは?

虫歯の治療をする歯医者のシーンでしょうか。患者である男性の視線に入ってくる、衛生
士女性のフェティッシュな仕草も面白い。でも僕、あれよりすごいものを見たことがある
んです。しかもキューバで。1994年のことで、メキシコ経由で日本からキューバに渡航
できるようになってからすぐのことでした。僕が知っている限りほかに現地に足を運んで
いる日本人は作家の村上龍さんくらい。彼はキューバ音楽に心酔していて、『ブエナ・ビ
スタ・ソシアル・クラブ』より早く日本にその魅力を伝えようとしていました。僕は当時
まだ編集者の仕事をしていたので雑誌の取材が目的でしたが、現地でひどい虫歯痛に悩ま
されて歯医者に駆け込んだんです。そうしたら歯科衛生士がドクターの愛人だったようで、
僕の治療をしながら濃密なキスを目の前で何度も繰り返すんです。あれはリアルな世界で
『タンポポ』を超えた経験でしたね(笑)。

Is it not the eroticism
that Itami also expressed in *Tampopo*?

Memories related to deliciousness also can't be expressed numerically.

That's why the people in *Tampopo* work so hard to find the perfect taste. I actually know one person who has synesthesia with taste. They could arrive at an unknown recipe just by taste memory like absolute pitch in music. What's different from music, however, is that the act of eating cannot be owned. The only way to enjoy the moment of eating is to use all five senses. I'm jealous because such synesthesia is a realm that AI can never reach. I often regret that I didn't go on the path of food.

What pleasure, if any, can surpass the activity of eating?

Is it not the eroticism that Itami also expressed in *Tampopo*? I sometimes think about the three primary human desires—food, sex, and sleep—but I know that in my dog's case, his appetite is greater than his desire for sleep because no matter how sleepy he looks, he comes running when I open a bag of snacks (laugh). I myself often make music with eroticism as a theme. It's a common thread that underlies not only music but all forms of entertainment. I think it's an important concept that stimulates human creativity.

What left a deep impression on you with regard to eroticism in Tampopo?

I guess the scene of a dentist treating a cavity. The fetishistic gestures of the female hygienist in the male patient's line of sight are also interesting. But I have seen something more impressive than that. And it was in Cuba. It was 1994, and shortly after it became possible to travel there from Japan via Mexico. The only other Japanese I knew who visited the area at the time was the writer Ryu Murakami. He was fascinated by Cuban music and wanted to introduce it to Japan. This was before the *Buena Vista Social Club*. I was still working as an editor then and went to do a magazine story, but in the country, I suffered from severe cavity pain and had to run to the dentist. The dental hygienist seemed to be the doctor's mistress, and they kissed intensely, again and again, while treating me. That was a real-world experience that went beyond *Tampopo* (laugh).

── DJ として世界を旅してもなお、東京の「食」のレベルは高く感じますか？

抜群に高く感じますよ。もちろんイタリアやスペイン、フランスなどのラテン系国家は歴
史もあるし、当然美味しい。でも僕らの味覚に関する身体能力ってどうしようもなく高い
から食べる側であるお客も、提供する側のお店も、双方のレベルが秀逸であることはすで
によく知られているんじゃないでしょうか。毎年パリ音楽祭で DJ のため現地を訪ねます
が、そこで知り合った何名かの日本人料理人たちがいました。きっと見習いの身と思いき
や、お店を訪ねてみるとオーナーシェフだったりするんです。ましてやフランス料理店の
ですよ。それってヒップホップの世界で例えるなら、ニューヨークのサウスブロンクスで
見たラップグループのリーダーが日本人だったとか、それくらいのレベル。僕個人として
は、彼らが作るような A 級の味をちゃんと知ったうえで、B 級の味にも精通していたい
と思うんです。両方を知っていてこそちゃんとした評価になると思うし、『タンポポ』が
食の映画として魅力的なのはまさに、A 級も B 級もどちらの"皿"もターンテーブルでミッ
クスするように、等しく映画の素材として調理していたからではないでしょうか。

Both A- and B-class "plates" equally as ingredients, like mixing on a turntable.

A級もB級もどちらの"皿"も
等しく映画の素材として
ターンテーブルでミックスするように、
調理していた

Even after traveling the world as a DJ, do you still feel that Tokyo's food is high quality?

Outstandingly high. Of course, food in Latin countries like Italy, Spain, and France has a history and is of course, delicious. However, it's well-known that since our physical abilities related to our sense of taste are quite advanced, both the customers doing the eating and the restaurants providing the food are at an excellent level in Tokyo. Every year I visit Paris to be a DJ at the Fête de la Musique, and I have met some Japanese chefs there. I thought they must be apprentices, but when I visited them at their restaurants, I found out that they were owner-chefs. And they are running a French restaurant. This would be like the leader of a rap group in the South Bronx in New York City being Japanese or something like that. Personally, after having a decent knowledge of the A-class flavors they create, I would also like to be well-versed in B-class flavors. Only by knowing both can one properly evaluate them. *Tampopo* is so appealing as a food film because it prepares both A- and B-class "plates" equally as ingredients, like mixing on a turntable.

― もしも自分が『タンポポ』のサウンドトラックを考えるならどうしますか？

『タンポポ』のサウンドトラックがクラシック音楽であることは有名だし、その効果ももちろんわかります。だから新しく代わる音楽が必要とは思わないし、音楽がないことも選択肢のひとつではないかと思います。

「無音に勝る音楽なし」

ただし、それは無音が許せる雰囲気が絶対条件になるでしょう。こだわりが強いお店であればこそ、いいお客として求められるマナーや暗黙の了解がある。そんな日本固有で独特とも言えるやりとりを通過して店主との間に結ばれる絆は、他のなにものにも替え難いですね。

田中知之（たなか・ともゆき）
音楽プロデューサー／選曲家

1997年に1stアルバム『The Fantastic Plastic Machine』以降、これまで計8枚のオリジナルアルバムやリミックスアルバム、ベストアルバムなどリリース。全米映画『オースティン・パワーズ：デラックス』や『SEX AND THE CITY』への楽曲提供の他、村上隆がルイ・ヴィトンの為に手掛けた短編アニメーション用の楽曲制作や、ユニクロのWEBコンテンツ『UNIQLOCK』では世界三大広告賞でそれぞれグランプリを受賞。DJとしては、国内の有名フェスは元より、米国のコーチェラ・フェスティバルやイギリスのレディング・フェスティバルなど海外の有名フェスへの出演経験も多数。豊富な音楽知識とセンスに裏打ちされたプレイスタイルで、多数のファッションブランドのパーティでのDJなど、クラブのみならず各方面で絶大な信頼を得ている。東京2020オリンピック開会式／閉会式、パラリンピック開会式では音楽監督を務めた。2022年度より洗足学園音楽大学"音楽・音響デザインコース"の客員教授に就任。

What would you put on a soundtrack for Tampopo?

As is well known, *Tampopo*'s soundtrack is classical music, and of course, I know how effective that is. So, I don't think we need new music to replace it. I think not having music is an option.

"There is no music better than silence."

However, it's absolutely necessary to have an atmosphere amenable to silence. If a restaurant is very particular about things, certain manners and unspoken understandings are expected of you as a good customer. It is hard to replace the bond formed between the customer and the owner through such interactions, which I think are unique to Japan.

Tomoyuki Tanaka
Music Producer / DJ

Since his first album, *The Fantastic Plastic Machine* came out in 1997, Tanaka has released eight original albums in addition to remix albums and best-of albums. He provided music for the U.S. films *Austin Powers: The Spy Who Shagged Me* and *Sex and the City*, and also created music for Takashi Murakami's animated short film for Louis Vuitton. The Uniqlo web project *Uniqlock*, which uses Tanaka's music, won grand prizes at the world's three major advertising award ceremonies. As a DJ, he has performed at many famous festivals in Japan and abroad, including Coachella in the United States and Reading in England. His DJing style, backed by a wealth of musical knowledge and sensibility, has earned him great trust in clubs and various other fields. For example, he has DJed at parties for numerous fashion brands. He was the musical director for the Tokyo 2020 Olympic Games Opening/Closing Ceremonies and the Paralympic Games Opening Ceremony. In 2022, he assumed the position of visiting professor for Senzoku Gakuen College of Music's Music Design Course.

You can eat it out of my hands.   **(laugh)   That tickles!**

Photograph_Yosuke Suzuki   Styling_Miwako Tanaka

Words of Outsiders

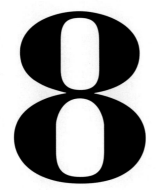

イノセンス　　Innocence

「アタイの手から食べるといいわ」

（笑）

「くすぐったい！」

「わたしの伯父さん」

長谷部千彩

大通り沿いにある大型書店。その日も私は棚の前に立ち、右から左へ、上から下へ、背表紙を舐めるように眺めていた。15歳、いや、16歳になっていたかもしれない。高校一年生だった。インターネットもスマートフォンもない時代、いまより少しだけ学生たちには余裕があった。退屈する時間があった。だから放課後、書店へ向かう。面白そうな本を探しては片っ端から読んでいた。使えるお金が少ないから、もっぱら買うのは文庫本。お気に入りは新潮文庫だ。背に並ぶ題字の端正な明朝体が好きだった。それから茶色の栞紐も。

一冊の本に目を留める。棚から引き抜き、裏表紙の解説を読む。ページをめくる。冒頭に置かれた一編は「スパゲッティのおいしい召し上がり方」。その茹で方について書いてある。日本人が食べているのはスパゲッティなどではない、炒め饂飩だ、と初っ端から手厳しい。今日はこれを読んでみるか。私はその本を手にレジへと向かった。タイトルは『女たちよ!』。伊丹十三という名は、その時知った。

隠すつもりもない。そのエッセイ集から私は多大な影響を受けている。スパゲッティの茹で方だけでなく、シャルル・ジュールダンの靴、フランス製のレースの下着、スポーツカーのハンドルの握り方。私が刺身を

食べる時、山葵を醤油に溶かず、直接刺身に載せるのも、シャネルの似合う女優というと真っ先にロミー・シュナイダーを思い浮かべるのも、たぶんその本による刷り込みだ。

伊丹十三は、日本人って奴は、と大袈裟姿に呆れてみせる。物知らぬ者たちを嗤う嫌味な「粋」や「洒落」や「本物」を彼の語りから学ぶのは、十代の私には刺激的だった。その訓えを、高校生の生真面目さでスポンジのごとく吸収した。この本が説くような享楽の世界に通じるために大人になることが必要ならば、早く大人になりたいものだ、そう思った。

それは導き――少女を大人にする導きだった。

大学に進学した私のまわりには、伊丹十三に影響を受けた男たちが大勢いた。当時、文化人として絶大な存在感を示していた伊丹十三に、彼らは私以上に心酔していた。物知りな、憧れの、伊丹十三は彼らにとってモノンクル、"ぼくの伯父さん"だった。

その頃、伊丹十三は、というと、劇場用映画を撮り始めていた。長編映画第一作『お葬式』、翌年には二作目にあたる『タンポポ』が公開された。もちろん私も封切りで観ている。続く三作目『マルサの女』が大

"My Uncle"

Chisai Hasebe

On the main street is a large bookstore. Again that day, I stand before its shelves, gazing greedily from right to left, from top to bottom, at the spines of the books. I am 15, or perhaps I have turned 16. I was in my first year of high school. With neither the internet nor smartphone, we had a little more time than students today. At times we were bored. Thus after school, I would head to the bookstore. If I found an interesting book, I would read it from cover to cover. As I didn't have much money, all I ever bought were paperbacks. My favorite were the Shincho Bunko paperbacks. I liked the line of well-defined Ming typeface lettering on the backs. And the brown bookmark strings as well.

My eye stops on a book. I pluck it from the shelf and read the commentary on the back cover. I turn the pages. It opens with a piece entitled "How to Eat Spaghetti so it Tastes Best." It explains the way to boil it. It is harsh in tone from the very beginning, saying that what the Japanese eat is not spaghetti but fried udon noodles. Shall I read this today? I take the book and head to the register. The title is *Listen, Women!* This is when I learn the name Juzo Itami.

I will speak plainly. This essay collection had an enormous influence on me. Not only on how to boil spaghetti, but Charles Jourdan shoes, French lace underwear, and how to hold the steering wheel of a sports car. The way I eat sashimi, putting the wasabi horseradish directly on the fish without first dissolving it in soy sauce, and having Romy Schneider come immediately to mind when I try to think of an actress who looks good in Chanel were probably both imprinted on me by this book.

Juzo Itami exaggerates how he is stunned by the stupidity of the Japanese people. He grumbles. While he could be overly sarcastic towards the ignorant, as a teenager I found what I learned from him about things neither my parents nor my teachers would tell me, such as "style," "refinement," or "truth," to be very stimulating. With the earnest sincerity of a high-school student, I soaked up these teachings like a sponge. If the road to adulthood led through the realm of pleasure upon which this book spoke as if in advocacy, I wanted to become an adult as quickly as possible. This was guidance—guiding a girl into womanhood.

Around me when I continued into university were many men who had been influenced by Juzo Itami. Their devotion to Itami, who was an enormous cultural figure by this time, was even greater than mine. Vastly knowledgeable and widely admired, for them, he was "mon oncle."

ヒット。彼は既に映画祭の常連監督になっていた。撮れば話題になる。賞を獲る。いつも紺色のマオカラーのジャケットを着ていた。その上に半纏を羽織っていることもあった。そのコーディネイトを、私は全く好きになれなかったけれど。おじいさんみたいだと思ったし、伊丹十三が着ればそれは洒落ていることになるという世間のへつらいのようなものも感じた。映画祭の受賞式の中継で、司会者に促され、トロフィーを手に作品の主演女優であり妻でもある宮本信子に感謝の言葉を捧げているのを観たことがある。一瞬、そこに家庭が垣間見え、鼻白んだ。エッセイを読んで、私はそこに伊丹十三のことを、ヨーロッパの香りがする男性、生活感のない男性なのだろうと勝手に想像していたから。伊丹十三は撮る映画よりも、書く文章のほうが好き。その気持ちはいまも変わらない。

伊丹十三の監督作品を観るために劇場に足を運んだのはいつまでだろう。『マルサの女2』『あげまん』『ミンボーの女』──その辺りから記憶が曖昧になる。観たような気もするし、観ていないような気もする。『静かな生活』は観たはずだ。自信はないが。

彼の作品から興味が逸れていったのは、私が大人になったからだと思う。指導教官から離れ、自分でハンドルを握り、私は自分の人生を走り出していた。伊丹十三のような年嵩の男たちは、もはや憧れの対象ではなくなっていた。彼らは私を女と見なし、性的な意味をもって近づいていた。時に彼らは私を落胆させ、私がその手を払いのけることもたびたびあった。

伊丹十三から受けた薫陶を忘れはしないが、私の中で存在は次第に薄れていった。それからしばらくして伊丹十三がこの世を去ったのは。まるで〝らしくない〟方法で。

デスクトップPCで『タンポポ』を再生する。観直すのは三十八年ぶり。

死んだ夫が残したラーメン屋をひとりで切り盛りする女。しかし店には閑古鳥が鳴いている。そこへ男が現れる。通りすがりのタンクローリー運転手。男は女に請われ、その店を繁盛させるべくひと肌脱ぐ、というのがあらすじ。その間に短いスケッチがいくつも挟まれる。食と生と性のコメディ。そう、コメディ映画なのだけれど、生理的嫌悪を覚え、あまり笑えなかったことを思い出す。例えばこのシーン──。

白いスーツ姿の男が岩場に腰を下ろし、煙草をくゆらせている。波間に海女が数人見える。男の視線が、

Around that time, Juzo Itami had begun to make feature films. He released his first full-length film, *The Funeral*, and the following year his second, *Tampopo*. Of course, I saw both at their premieres. His third, *A Taxing Woman*, was a smash hit. He had become a regular director at film festivals. People talked about everything he filmed. He won prizes. He always wore a navy-blue Mao jacket. Over it were a short Hanten jacket and a formal Haori coat. I didn't like this outfit at all, though. I thought he looked like an old man, and when people said Juzo Itami dressing this way made it stylish, I felt as if they were simply flattering him. I saw him in a film festival awards broadcast, urged on by the MC, with a trophy in his hands dedicating words of thanks to his lead actress and wife, Nobuko Miyamoto. For a second, I caught a glimpse of him as if at home, and I was disappointed. In reading his essays, I had imagined Juzo Itami as a man with the scent of Europe about him, one without a quotidian, everyday life. More than his movies, I liked his writing. That feeling has not changed.

How long has it been since I went to a theater to see a film directed by Juzo Itami? *A Taxing Woman's Return, Tales of a Golden Geisha, Minbo*—my memory goes hazy around that point. I feel like I've seen them, and I feel like I haven't. I have reason to think I've seen *A Quiet Life*, but I'm not sure.

I think it was because I had become an adult that I lost interest in his films. I broke away from my advisor, took the steering wheel myself, and set out to live my own life. Elders like Juzo Itami were no longer the objects of my admiration. They looked down on me as a woman and tried to get close to me with sex on their minds. Sometimes they would make me depressed, and I often thrust their hands away.

Although I never forgot the lessons I had learned from Juzo Itami, they grew fainter within me with time. And then it was a while later. Juzo Itami departed this world. In a way that did not suit him at all.

On my desktop computer, I replay *Tampopo*. I'm seeing it again after 38 years.

Alone, a woman is running the ramen restaurant her late husband left her. But the restaurant is empty. Now a man appears, a passing tank-truck driver. The story is about how the man, asked by the woman, makes an effort and helps her make the restaurant prosper. Interspersed are a number of short sketches and comedies of food, life, and sex. Yes, the film is a comedy, but I remember a visceral

海から上がってくる年若い海女の姿を捉える。幼さが残る美しい面立ち。男は娘に、採った牡蠣を見せてくれと頼む。魚籠の中から取り出される立派な牡蠣。娘は器用に殻をこじ開け、男に渡す。と、その身を食そうと口を近づける。と、その瞬間、上唇に真っ赤な血が滲む。殻の端で切ったのだ。娘は男の手から牡蠣を取り戻すと、今度はナイフを入れて身を外し、自らの手のひらに載せて差し出す。

「あたいの手から食べるといいわ」

男は娘の手をつかみ引き寄せて、その手のひらに唇を寄せる。そして音を立てて白い身を啜る。意味ありげな娘の瞳。娘は顔を近づけ、男の唇に浮かぶ血を舐める。何度も何度も。男と娘は舌を伸ばし合い、からませあう。海女たちがそんな二人を遠くから見ている。

孤独な男が蠱惑的な少女に出会う。性的魅力を無自覚に振りまく少女に誘惑される。それは男たちの一つの夢の形。文学が、映画が、繰り返し取り上げてきた古典的なファンタジーだ。かつての文学少女たちは、そのファンタジーに親しんできた。私もそのひとり。ファンタジーのよき理解者になり、イノセントな少女という役を引き受け、共演を務めてきた。時代もそんな男たちの夢想を庇っていたと思う。それがいつから

だろう、変わり始めたのは。女も、男も、社会も、私も。

とどのつまり、イノセントなのは、娘たちではなく、男たちだったのだ。

娘たちはやがて女になり、大人になる。そして気づく。男たちの頭から抜け落ちている、あることに。男が娘たちを眼差す時、娘たちもまた男をじっと見ている。冷徹に批評している。なのになぜ、男たちは共有した時間が娘にとっても甘やかなものであるはずと信じきっているのか。意味ありげな瞳に、意味など宿っていないかもしれないのに。

劇中、宮本信子演じる主人公は、おぼこい女として描かれる。健気で無知で無教養。「(私は)えらい?」──自分を褒めて、と甘える言葉はまるで小学生だ。

男たちはエキスパートという立場から皆で彼女を教育する。彼女は彼らに頼り、努め、ラーメンを完成させる。満面の笑顔。得意気で──。そして男たちは去っていく。女を育てあげたという愉悦を胸に。『タンポポ』は古典的ウエスタン映画を踏襲しているだけではない。古典的なセクシュアルファンタジーの系譜にもあると思う。

disgust at which I found it hard to laugh. For example, in this scene:

A man in a white suit sits on some rocks, smoking a cigarette. In the ocean waves, we see some pearl divers. A young girl diver emerging from the water catches his eye. She is beautiful, her features still those of a child. The man asks her to show him an oyster she has caught. From her creel, she takes out a magnificent oyster. She skillfully pries open the shell and gives it to the man. He raises it to his mouth to eat. Then, at that moment, red blood oozes from his upper lip. The oyster shell has cut him. The girl takes the oyster from the man's hand, takes it out of the shell with her knife, and holds it out to him in the palm of her hand.

"You can eat it out of my hands."

The man grasps the girl's hand and pulls it to him, pressing his lips to her palm. Loudly he slurps up the white meat. The girl brings her face close to his. She licks the blood on his lip. Again and again. The man and the girl extend their tongues and entwine them. The other divers watch the two from a distance away.

A lone man meets an alluring young girl. He is enticed by her air of innocent sexuality. This is a man's dream. A classic fantasy repeatedly depicted in novels and films. In the past, young girls who loved literary works were familiar with such fantasy. I was one of them. I sympathized with this fantasy, took on the role of an innocent young girl, and performed it. The times were protecting this men's fantasy. When did that begin to change, I wonder. Among women, men, society, and me.

In the end, it was not the girls who were innocent; it was the men.

In time girls become women and then adults. Then they realize something. Something that has been left out of men's heads. When men watch girls, the girls watch back with coolly critical eyes. So why do men fool themselves into believing that the time they share is also an unalloyed sweetness for her? Her eyes may be suggestive, but there may not be any meaning to that.

In the movie, the central character played by Nobuko Miyamoto is portrayed as childish. She is admirable, ignorant, and uneducated. "(Am I) that great?" This self-indulgence makes her sound like an elementary school girl.

授乳のシーンで映画は終わる。私はデスクを離れ、コーヒーを淹れる。この映画が放つ、強烈な80年代の匂いにため息をつく。ヤバい、ウザい、キモい、という言葉を娘たちが獲得する前の時代。その言葉が破壊したものについても考える。

2023年、娘たちは伯父さんの導きなど必要とはしていない。私は伯父さんを慕う最後の娘なのかもしれない。だとすれば、少し寂しくも思う。男たちにとって "ぼくの伯父さん" であったように、私にとっても、彼は物知りな、憧れの、"わたしの伯父さん" だった。

そんな伯父さんが、いま、時代から取り残されてしまったように見える。

男が女を導こうとするならば、モラハラ！と糾弾される。女が男に導かれたいと願うなら、自分でググれよ！と突き放される。エロティシズムが立ちのぼる隙などそこにはない。導く男も導かれる女も存在しない世界。この先、尋ねたら答えてくれるのはAIになるらしい。

時の流れは残酷だ。けれど、こうも思うのだ。それは悪いことだろうか。ワクワクしながら聞いた蘊蓄を鬱陶しく感じるようになった私の成長は嘆かわしいことだろうか。あの頃よりも女にとって時代はずっとずっとマシなものになっている。

年をとったからわかる。時代が変わったからわかる。私もイノセントだったけど、伯父さんも相当イノセントだったのね。

80年代は遠い昔。時間は不可逆。イノセントな季節は戻ってこない。だから、ここでお別れしましょう。

私は苦いコーヒーをふくむ。苦い苦いコーヒーを。

さようなら、伯父さん。

さようなら、白いスーツを着た "わたしの伯父さん"。

長谷部千彩（はせべ・ちさい）
文筆家

エッセイの他、掌編小説、映像作品のシナリオ、広告コピーなど幅広く執筆。著書に『私が好きなあなたの匂い』『メモランダム』（河出書房新社）、『有閑マドモワゼル』（光文社知恵の森文庫）等がある。ウェブマガジン≪memorandom≫主宰。https://hasebechisai.com/

From the position of expert, the men all educate her. They share her. She looks up to them, depends on them, works hard, and succeeds at making ramen. She smiles with her whole face. She is good at this. And then the men leave, their hearts full of the pleasure of having educated a woman. *Tampopo* does more than follow the classic western movie. I think it is also in the lineage of a classic sexual fantasy.

The film ends with a breastfeeding scene. I removed the disc and made some coffee. I heaved a sigh at the strong smell of the '80s the film gives off. It was before women gained expressions like "Crap!" or "Annoying!" or "Gross!" I also thought about what these words have destroyed.

In 2023, girls do not need the leadership of older uncles. I am perhaps the last one who did. If this is true, I also feel a little bereft. Just as the boys saw "mon oncle" in Itami, I also saw a knowledgeable and admirable "uncle" in him. But now that uncle seems left behind in the times.

If a man tries to guide a woman, he will be accused, "That's mora-hara(moral harassment)!" If a woman wants to be guided by a man, she will be shunned and told to "just google it!" Here there is no opportunity for eroticism to arise. This is a world in which there are no men who lead and no women who are led. From now on, it seems, it will be AI that answers when asked.

The passage of time is merciless. However, is this really such a bad thing? Is it lamentable that I have grown up to feel gloomy about hearing the knowledge I used to listen to with excitement? For women, the times now are far, far better than they were back then.

Since I have gotten older, I understand.

Because the times have changed, I understand.

I was innocent, but so was the old uncle.

The '80s are far in the past.

Time does not flow backward.

The season of innocence will not return.

So let us part ways here.

I sip on my bitter coffee.

Goodbye, "my uncle."

Goodbye, my uncle in the white suit.

Translation_Ian MacDougall

Chisai Hasebe
Writer

Hasebe writes in various fields, including essays along with short novels, film scenarios, and advertising copy. Her works include *The Smell of You that I Like* (Kawade Shobo Shinsha) and *Leisure Madamoiselle* (Kobunsha Chie No Mori Bunko). She also runs the web magazine "memorandum." https://hasebechisai.com/

臨海地域を持つ都市部に幾重にも入り込む電車や線路の様相
は、都市という大きなどんぶりに入り込む麺の様相そのものだ。
（P152『近代都市と痛み』 ヴィヴィアン佐藤）

The appearance of cities with coastal areas threaded through with layers
of trains and tracks have the aspect of noodles introduced into a donburi
rice-bowl dish. (P153 "Pain and the Modern City" by Vivian Sato)

9

Photograph_Yusuke Komiyama (mobiile)   Model_Vivian Sato

ポストモダン　Postmodern

「アンタ、自分で匂いませんでした？」

「え？」

「死ぬかと思ったよ。ありゃ、くせぇんだ」

Didn't you smell it?

Huh?

I thought I'd die from the smell.

「近代都市と痛み」

ヴィヴィアン佐藤

伊丹十三監督の『タンポポ』という奇妙な作品は、誰をも拒絶しないエンターテインメント作品であることは間違いないが、一方では監督自身における「映画や夢とは一体何であるのか」という自己言及的かつ自己批評的な映像論にもなっている。その映像論は伊丹の結論として帰結するのではなく、問題提起そのものとして観客に差し出され、回答は観客に委ね試される。

関連のないサイドストーリーと呼ばれる幾つかのエピソード群が突然挿入されるのも特徴だ。演者の一人が我々観客と同じ立場・目線からカメラを直視し、我々に直接問いかけてくる。寺山修司が幾度も実験していたように、それは物理的なスクリーンを境に鏡像関係のようなメタ構造を成しており、その演者がいつの間にか映画の中の一出演者となって物語に回収されてしまったり、実に重層的な構造でもある。そして視点は鳥瞰的であり虫瞰的、構造的であり表層的、聖と俗、豊かさと貧しさ、生理と理性、虚構と現実など対立極を滑らかに往復する。

さて、劇中最も奇妙かつ強烈なサイドストーリーで、藤田敏八が演じる歯髄壊疽を患い猛烈な歯痛に苦しむ男のエピソードがある。男がイヤホンを耳に付け一人

Pain and the Modern City

Vivian Sato

It is no mistake to say that *Tampopo*, this curious work of the director Juzo Itami, is undeniably an entertainment film. Still on the other hand, it is a motion-picture theory of self-reference and self-questioning, in which the director asks, "What are things like movies or dreams?" Itami does not draw a conclusion; he poses the question and leaves it to the audience to answer.

Another characteristic of the film is the sudden insertion of the unrelated so-called "side-story" group of episodes. One of the actors faces the camera in the same position and sight line as the audience and speaks directly to us. Just as the avant-garde artist Shuji Terayama experimented with on numerous occasions, this is a multi-layered structure, a meta-construction making the limits of the screen into something like a mirror image with the actor suddenly swept up as a player in the story. The point of view shifts smoothly between opposites, such as bird's-eye and insect's-eye, structural and superficial, holy and profane, richness and poverty, physiological and logical, and fiction and truth.

The strangest and most compelling of the movie's

電車に乗っていると、急に歯痛に襲われる。そこに突然電車の中で登場し点心を提供する中国人美少女が、男に自前の点心をテーブル上に満面の笑顔で支給する。男の歯痛はますます酷くなり、男は電車を降りて歯医者へと駆け込む。

歯医者の施術椅子に座らせられた男は、男性の医師と二人の看護婦により治療を受ける。さまざまな先端を有する手術用でステンレス製の精密な歯科器具はメタリックに輝き、フェティッシュ感の極地だ。それらは昨今では若者の間で市民権を得ている鼻ピアスや眉ピアスに使用されるアクセサリー素材と同一だ。そして幾つもの器具や注射器を使用し、やはりステンレス製のサイドテーブルに粗野に置かれる際に放たれる金属音。そして治療中には吸引機やドリルの機械音が鳴り響く。施術椅子にがんじがらめに座らせられ、身動きできない状態の身体感覚は、言語を奪い、視覚と触覚とが鋭敏に研ぎ澄まされた領域に追いやられる。男は施術用の強烈なライトで目を一杯には開けられず、その分、看護婦の視線や彼女らの施術服から覗く脇しか目に入らなくなる。身動きができない分、動かせる足先や看護婦の生脚が当たる身体箇所だけが極めて敏感になる。痛みとライトの熱により男の額には大粒の

汗が噴出し続ける。もちろん大量の涎も噴出しているだろう。施術の後半に口内の壊疽部分から強烈な異臭が放たれ、歯医者と看護婦二人は我慢できず窓から深呼吸をする。ここまではほとんど会話という会話無しの無声の展開で、それは冒頭に男がイヤホンを付けて外の世界とは聴覚的に遮断している所以であろう。

この作品は伊丹十三による映画論でもあると述べたが、死に際に見る最後の映画、つまり走馬灯のように生前見てきた現実や映画が駆け抜ける経験が、人間にとって最後の映画であると登場人物に語らせる。またこの作品は伊丹が今まで過去に見てきた映画、いわゆる映画史の引用に満ちている。この『タンポポ』という作品は、伊丹自身が見てきた映画、経験してきた光景が、走馬灯のように展開していくのだ。

この歯痛の男のエピソードは、谷崎潤一郎原作小説の『白日夢』からの引用で、鬼才・武智鉄二が三度に渡り映画化に挑んだ執念の作品群へのオマージュであろう。『白日夢』では主人公の貧乏画家が、ビルの6階にある歯科医の二つ並んだ施術椅子に座らせられ、もう一方には美貌の流行歌手が施術椅子に座らせられ、施術を受けている。医者はクロロホ

人公は麻酔を打たれ意識朦朧となる。

side stories is the man's episode, played by Toshiya Fujita, who suffers the agonizing pain of tooth gangrene. Alone on a train, with an earphone, the man is assailed by toothache. Then suddenly, a beautiful Chinese girl appears on the train and offers dim sums with a big smile on her face. His toothache worsens, and he leaves the train and goes to the dentist.

Seated in the chair, the man is treated by the male dentist and two female nurses. Sharp-pointed stainless-steel precision dental tools with various tips give off a metallic shine and are the ultimate fetish. These materials are the same as those used for nose and eyebrow piercing, which are widely accepted among young people nowadays. And after any number of these instruments and injections, they give off a metallic clank when placed randomly on a metallic side table. The sounds of the suction machine and the drill reverberate during the procedure. Seated firmly down in the dentist's chair, unable to move or speak, the man is driven into a situation where his senses of vision and touch are rendered very sharp. Under the powerful lighting, he is unable to fully open his eyes, and all he is able to see are the nurses' eyes and their armpits peeking through their white dresses. Because he cannot move his body, he is extremely sensitive to his toes and the parts of him that contact the nurses' bare legs. With the pain and the heat of the lights, large drops of sweat pour from his forehead. Late in the operation, the gangrene gives off a powerful stench that is too much for the dentist and the nurses, who gasp for breath from a window.

To this point, the scene is as if it were from a silent movie, with no conversation worthy of the name. This is probably because the man wears earphones at the beginning of the sequence and is aurally cut off from the outside world.

I have said that this movie serves as a Juzo Itami theory of film, but through the characters, he says that on the point of death, all the memories or scenes of a lifetime that flash in front of one's eyes will form a film, the last that one sees. Also, this work is every film Itami has ever seen, meaning that it is full of references to movie history. In *Tampopo*, all the movies Itami has seen and all the sights he has experienced play out as if on a magic lantern.

The man with the toothache episode references *Daydream*, a story by Junichiro Tanizaki. We can assume that it is an homage to the obsessive movies of the brilliant director Tetsuji Takechi, who took

ルムで歌手の意識を失わせ、彼女の肉体を犯す。また、主人公はナイトクラブで歌手を助け出そうと訪ねるが、そこに再び医師が現れる。場面は変わり歌手はすでに屍体となっており、気が付けば自分が血まみれのナイフを持って刑事に逮捕。その瞬間、歯医者の施術椅子にいまだに座っている自分に気付くのだ。その一瞬の走馬灯の光景が夢だったというものである。

壊死に至る激痛で意識が朦朧とし、電車内の中国人少女が果たして現実なのか妄想なのか。術後、医師から柔らかい物から食すよう論され、屋外でソフトクリームを食べる男。傍らには「自然食以外のオヤツやお菓子は与えないで欲しい」という母親からの札を付けた幼児が佇んでいる。男は幼児に向かって自分の食べかけのソフトクリームを差し出し、躊躇はするものの、幼児は美味しそうにソフトクリームにしゃぶりつき病みつきになってしまう。これはキリスト教のアダムとイヴが犯した罪、いわゆる原罪の隠喩だろう。歯痛の男は幼児にとっては、神への裏切りをそそのかしイヴを騙した蛇なのだ。砂糖が含まれている甘い菓子類には中毒性や依存性があり、健康を害する可能性のあるドラッグのようなものかも知れない。

『タンポポ』において歯痛の男の壊死部から強烈な悪臭が放たれ、医師たちが我慢することが出来ず咄嗟にビルの上階の窓を開けて深呼吸をする。ここから飛躍して、近代=モダニズムにおいて、高層ビルや建物を都市における「歯」と解釈することが出来ないだろうか。もしくは人工のインプラントといえばもっと臨場感があるかも知れない。歯茎から伸びてくる神経はそれぞれの一個ずつの歯には対応していない。虫歯の場合、虫歯の箇所の部分だけが痛みが伴うとは限らないのである。神経は歯茎の中では枝分かれをしており、近代=モダニズムの諸問題は、世界は均一空間であることが大前提で、固有の場所性は問われない。そのことから都市に建てられるビルはそこにある存在の必然性が希薄になるのである。

『タンポポ』に登場する最上階に歯医者が構えられている白い高層ビルは、都市における歯そのもので、歯痛の男の壊死部分が開かれ悪臭を放つと同時に、都市の歯の上層部（＝窓）が解放されるのである。そこには入れ子構造が成り立つ。歯痛の男の身体は近代の身体そのものだということになる。嗜好品としてのお菓子やオヤツは、栄養を摂取するためのものではない現代の甘い毒でもある。中毒性や依存性のあるお菓子

on its filming three times. In *Daydream*, a poverty-stricken writer sits in one of two dentist chairs in a 6th-floor office while being treated in the other is a beautiful popular woman singer. The main character is given anesthetic and rendered semi-conscious. The dentist renders the singer unconscious with chloroform and sexually assaults her. The hero then visits a nightclub to try and help the singer, but the dentist appears again. The scene changes, the singer is now dead, and the man realizes he is holding a bloody knife and being arrested by a detective. At that moment, he realizes he is still sitting in the dentist's chair. That scene that flashed in an instant before his eyes was a dream.

For the man rendered semi-conscious by the intense pain that leads to necrosis, is the Chinese girl on the train real or a fantasy? The dentist warns him to begin with soft things to eat, so he eats a soft-cream cone outside. A boy standing beside him bears a note from his mother that reads, "I do not wish this child fed snacks or sweets that are not natural." The man turns to the boy and holds out his soft scream. The child hesitates, licks eagerly at the cone, and cannot stop. This is probably a metaphor for the original sin of Adam and Eve in Christianity. For the boy, the man with the toothache is the snake who deceived Eve by instigating her betrayal of God. Sweet confectionery products that contain sugar may be toxic and addictive and may be like drugs that can be harmful to health.

The decayed portion of the man's tooth in *Tampopo* gives off a powerful stench, and unable to stand it, the dentist and the others open a window on the upper floor of the building and inhale deeply. Leaping forward from here, can we not, according to the tenets of modernism, interpret skyscrapers and buildings as the "teeth" of the city? Describing them as artificial implants might give more of a sense of realism. Nerves coming from the gums do not correspond exactly to individual teeth. Where tooth pain is felt may not be limited to where a cavity is located. Nerves branch throughout the gums and are not localized. The issues of modernism are premised on the world being a single unified space, and the unique sense of place goes unexamined. Because of this, buildings in cities have little necessity to exist at a specific location.

The tall white building with the dentist's office on its top floor is itself a tooth in the big city, and as the foul smell of the man's gangrenous tooth is released, the upper part of the city tooth—the

に毒された身体や身体感覚は、元には戻れないこともも暗示されているようだ。英語圏のモダニスト作家のジェイムス・ジョイスは若い頃から虫歯に苦しみ、それが原因で晩年は眼病になった。『ユリシーズ』では意識の流れを多用した小説で有名だが、『タンポポ』もまた伊丹の脳内の意識の流れといったものを感じないこともない。

最後に付け加えておきたいことは、歯痛の男が登場するシーンについてだ。白服の男が牡蠣の海女とのシーンの背景で疾走している電車が確認できるが、歯痛の男はその電車に乗っていたようなシークエンスとなっている。この作品全編に渡り昼夜問わず電車がひたすら走る。

線路という鉄でできたレールは、どこまでも延びて進んでいくというイメージのもので、モダニズムの象徴とも取れるものだ。鉄という均一な素材は建材にしろ土木にしろ都市の風景を一変させた。また臨海地域を持つ都市部に幾重にも入り込む電車や線路の様相は、都市という大きなどんぶりに入り込む麺の様相そのものだ。もしくは都市という脳内に入り込む神経細胞だ。そうなるとゴローが運転する愛用のトラックは、

やはり同じ鉄製ではあるが、自由に動き回ることができる焼豚といったところか。物語に急に貫入してくる歯痛の男の登場は、物理的にも都市に貫入してくる電車でなければならなかったのだ。そして神経回路から都市に入り込んだ男は、最終的にビルの最上階から解放される現代の「痛み」の象徴なのかも知れない。

ポストモダンの都と呼ばれ、ポストモダンと相性が良過ぎたバブル期の日本とは。

大きな物語を背景に持つモダニズムではなく、懐疑的で折衷的、かつ分裂的なポストモダン。

様々な文化や価値観が流れ着くアジアの果てとしての日本。

そこのどんぶりの中には都市や宇宙、作法や生き様がぎっしりと詰まっていた。

ヴィヴィアン佐藤（ゔぃゔぃあん・さとう）
非建築家／美術家／ドラァグクイーン／誤読の女王

都市や映画をあらゆる角度で読み解こうとするアーティスト。最近のモットーは「垂直に旅する。 都市も芸術もそれを計画し製作した者の所有物ではなく、旅行者や鑑賞者も同等に責任を負わねばならない」。大正大学客員教授。

ポストモダン

window—is set free. This creates a nesting structure. The body of the man with a toothache is the very body of modernity. Sweets and treats as luxury items are not a source of nutrition but a sweet poison of modernity. There is a hint here that the body and its sensations, poisoned by the toxic addictiveness of sweets, are past the point of no return. The modernist writer James Joyce was troubled from his youth by toothache, which in later years affected his eyesight. *Ulysses* is famous as a novel that depicts streams of consciousness, and in *Tampopo*, one can also slightly feel the stream of Itami's consciousness.

What I would like to add at the end concerns the scene in which the man with a toothache appears. In the scene of the man in the white suit and the oyster diver, a train can be seen in the background. The sequence positions the man with the toothache on this train. Day and night, trains run continuously through this film.

As an image of something leading on forever, the iron rails called tracks can be taken as a symbol of modernism. Iron, which is the same everywhere, has brought a complete change to the face of the city, whether as a building material or in public works. The appearance of cities with coastal areas threaded through with layers of trains and tracks have the aspect of noodles introduced into a donburi rice-bowl dish. Or they are nerve cells in that city called the brain. If this is so, is Goro's beloved truck, similarly made of iron, a slice of fried pork that can float around freely in the ramen bowl? The appearance of the man with the toothache that suddenly penetrated the story had to be on a train that physically penetrated the city. And the man entering the city through its neural network may symbolize the pain of modernity, finally released on the top floor of one of its buildings.

What was Japan during the bubble period when it was called the capital of post-modernism, with which it got along so well ?

It was not modernism with a whole story behind it but a skeptical, compromising, and ultimately divisive post-modernism.

Japan exists at the far end of Asia, where various cultures and values flow in and out.

That donburi bowl was stuffed with cities, universes, manners, and ways of life.

Translation_Ian MacDougall

Vivian Sato
Non-Architect / Artist / Drag Queen / Queen of Misreading

Sato is an artist who reads cities or movies from every angle. Her current motto is "Travel vertically. Neither cities nor art belongs to those who created them, and travelers and spectators must bear equal responsibility." She is also Visiting Professor at Taisho University.

Akiko Kikuchi

菊 池 亜 希 子

Voices of Outsiders

女優さんから『タンポポ』の話を聞くなら、自分と同世代が好ましい。小さな頃に味わった異物感と今観ることで得る新鮮さを比較できるし、食いしん坊であれば余計にいい。ラーメンの魅力ではなく、食べることへの魅力を追求した映画として語ってもらえるから。本件における食いしん坊の定義は、グルメでも大食いでもなく、食べることを慈しめること。だからその名も『おなかのおと』（文藝春秋）という著書まで執筆している菊池亜希子は、格好の候補だった。

「別に詳しいわけじゃない」と躊躇する彼女に、改めて『タンポポ』を観たうえで取材の是非を検討してもらいたいと自らハードルを上げたオファーは、検討期間を一拍おいて了承を得ることができた。

4

今観ることに価値がある。更に観てしまったらもっと発見がある。そんな大事なことはもっと早く言ってほしかったのに、伊丹十三は今もどこかで飄々と我々の先を歩いている。その背中を遠目に追いながら、渋谷の焼肉屋でこの取材に臨んだのだ。

If you want to hear about *Tampopo* from an actress, she should preferably be of the same generation as yourself. You can compare the foreign feeling you experienced when you were little with the freshness you get from watching it now. It's even better if she's a foodie–she can talk about the film as being about what's great about eating, not the appeal of ramen. "Foodie" here means neither a gourmand nor glutton, but rather one who cherishes eating. Therefore, Akiko Kikuchi, who has even written a book entitled *The Sound of My Stomach* (*Onaka no Oto*; Bungeishunju Ltd.), was a good candidate.

She hesitated, saying, "I'm not an expert on that film." I asked her to watch *Tampopo* again and consider whether or not she would be interested–raising the bar even higher for an interview offer–but she agreed after some consideration.

It is worth watching now. If you watch it more, you will discover more. I wish I had been told such an important thing earlier, but Juzo Itami is still wandering ahead of us. I followed his back from afar to conduct this interview at a yakiniku restaurant in Shibuya.

Interview_Makoto Miura (COLAXO)
Photographs_Takahiro Otsuji (Nitoland)
Styling_Yumeno Ogawa
Hair & Make Up_Hiroko Takashiro
Translation_Trivector Co., Ltd.

特にそれぞれのサイドストーリーからは

普遍的な要素を感じました。

— 今改めて『タンポポ』を観ると、昔とは印象が変わりましたか？

大学生の頃に日本映画を片っ端から観た時があって、その時の印象は奇抜で生々しくて、決して心地よいものではありませんでした。でも今改めて観ると、特にそれぞれのサイドストーリーからは普遍的な要素を感じました。日本人の食べることに関する原体験のような、日本人なら誰もが記憶に残している風景のような。昭和の時代感も後押ししているかもしれないですね。

— 喫茶店をはじめ、昭和の文化がお好きですよね？

もともと自分が実際に生きている時代よりも、少し前の時代に惹かれる傾向がありました。特に昭和からあるような喫茶店にはあの時代の空気を感じ、そこに居た人の営みを想像することができる。なにより落ち着くんです。懐古主義にはなりたくないですけれど、おばあちゃんっ子であんこ好きだし、小さい頃住んでいたのは団地で、チャルメラの音が聞こえたらどんぶりを抱えて屋台を追いかけていたような、昭和の記憶が自分の歴史にはちゃんと刻まれていますから。

I felt universal elements, especially from each side story.

When you watch Tampopo again now, do you have a different impression than you did in the past?

When I was a university student and watched every Japanese film I could get my hands on, my impression was that it was bizarre, graphic, and certainly not pleasant. But watching it again now, I felt universal elements, especially from each side story. They're like the original food-related experiences of Japanese people, scenes that are in every Japanese person's memory. The Showa period atmosphere may have also helped.

You like Showa-era culture, including coffee shops, don't you?

I have always been attracted to the eras a little earlier than the one in which I actually live. Especially in coffee shops that have been around since the Showa period, one can feel the atmosphere of that era and imagine the activities of the people who were there at the time. Above all, it calms me down. I don't want to be nostalgic, but I am a grandma's girl and love anko (red bean paste), and I lived in a public apartment complex as a child. My memories of the Showa period—such as chasing after a food vendor with a bowl when I heard their distinctive suona instrument sounds—are etched in my history.

—— 菊池さんのエッセイでは、記憶に食べ物がよく紐づきますね

著書である『おなかのおと』は、幼少期の思い出と食べ物に纏わる記憶が結びついている
エピソードがたくさんあります。あの中で記した「への字スパゲッティ」は私の人生におい
て"おいしい"の原体験と言えます。記憶に残るしょうゆ味のスパゲッティと、自分の
頑固さが原因で記憶できなかったミートソースに関するエピソード。私の"おいしい"に
関する思い出は、その時の食べ物がおいしかったかどうかっていうことよりむしろ、食べ
る行為をフィルターにして浮かんでくる自分の歴史と言えるかもしれません。

—— 出演されている映画の中でも、食べ物が印象的な作品があります

主演として2作目だった『ファの豆腐』は実際の豆腐屋さんで撮影されましたが、食べ物
を取り扱う営みそのものだけで映像が雄弁になり、映画として成立することを実感しまし
たし、よしもとばななさん原作の『海のふた』では人生に悩んだのち、かき氷屋を切り盛
りしながら新しい生き方を模索する主人公を演じました。小津安二郎作品然り、食べ物を
通じたコミュニケーションってどこか日本映画的だなって思うんです。箸が進むか進ま
ないかがキャラクターの心象風景を代弁したり、食べ物があるだけで映像として観客の気持
ちを引き込みやすい。『タンポポ』もそうですよね。オムライスがおいしそうに見えるこ
とも大切だけれど、それを取り扱うホームレスたちの生き方が魅力的に映ったり。食を通
じて描かれる人間の滑稽さ、おかしさみたいなものがすべてのサイドストーリーの中で通
奏低音として流れているように感じます。

In your essays, food is often tied to memories.

My book, *The Sound of My Stomach*, is full of episodes that connect childhood reminiscences with memories associated with food. The spaghetti that I wrote about in my book is my touchstone experience of "deliciousness." Perhaps one could say that my memories of deliciousness—an episode about soy sauce spaghetti that remains in my memory and a meat sauce that I couldn't remember because of my stubbornness—are not so much about whether the food was good or not but rather about my own history that comes to mind through the act of eating.

Among the films in which you have appeared, there are ones in which the food leaves an impression.

In my second film as a leading actress, *Fa no Tofu*, which was shot in an actual tofu shop, I realized that the mere act of handling food itself makes the images eloquent and makes the footage work as a film. In *There Is No Lid on the Sea*, based on a book by Banana Yoshimoto, I played the main character who, after struggling with life, seeks a new way to live while running a shaved ice shop. Communication through food, as in the works of Yasujiro Ozu, is somewhat typical of Japanese cinema. Whether or not a character eats a little or a lot can speak for their emotional landscape, and the mere presence of food in an image can easily draw in the audience's feelings. The same is true of *Tampopo*. The omelet must look delicious, but how the homeless people who handle it live out their lives is also wonderful. The funny and ridiculousness of human beings, portrayed through food, is a common thread that runs through all side stories in the movie.

— 主演の宮本信子さんの演技はどのように感じましたか？

とってもチャーミングですよね。ただそれ以上に伊丹さんの「ウチの奥さん綺麗だろ！？」っていう声が聞こえてきそうなくらい、宮本さんへの愛を感じてしまいました。うちは夫婦で仕事をすることがないから羨ましいくらい。でも夫婦じゃなくても、例えばモデルとカメラマンの関係性だったらシャッターを切る瞬間、疑似恋愛のような感情が滲み出ることってあると思うんですけれど、そういう感覚って案外大事。血が通っていない褒め言葉っていうものに、撮られる側は案外敏感なので（笑）。

伊丹さんの「ウチの奥さん綺麗だろ！？」
っていう声が聞こえてきそう

— 多面的な活動をされている側面は伊丹監督と似ているように思えます

いやいや、そんなことはありませんけれど、女優やモデル以外にも、イラストを描いたり、文章を書いたり、雑誌を編集したりと、いろんなジャンルのお仕事をさせていただいているのは、すべてはいい出会いがあって、周りがいい風をもってきてくれたからできたことなんです。もともとゼロからなにかを生み出せるバイタリティーがあるわけじゃない。でもいつもいいタイミングで"こんなことやってみない？"って声をかけていただいて、「自分に出来ることがあるなら応えたい」と思ってやってきた結果、という感じです。なんの根拠もなく新しいチャレンジを促される理由はわかりませんが、そう言ってもらえるのはやっぱり嬉しいですね。

— 大学は建築科だったらしいですね

だから『タンポポ』が最後にリニューアルした様子には、"もしかしてピスケンが暴走した？"と勝手な想像をしてしまいました。一気通貫していた昭和の世界観が、いきなりモダンになりましたから。バブル前の好景気の世相があのインテリアに導いたんでしょうね。個人的には元々のお店も味わいがあって好きでしたが、古きものに感謝しすぎるのは現代人や都会人のエゴかもしれないですよね。地元にショッピングモールができると「あぁ、またか…」と上京民は無責任にセンチメンタルに浸ったりしますけど、地元の人はやっぱり喜びますから。それぞれの時代、それぞれの環境になにが相応しくて、なにが悪いのかって、やっぱり時間が経ってみないとわからないですよね。

What did you think of Nobuko Miyamoto's performance in the lead role?

Very charming, no? But more than that, I could almost hear Itami's voice saying, "My wife is beautiful, isn't she!?" My husband and I never work as a couple, so it almost makes me jealous. But even if you are not a married couple, if you are a model and a photographer, for example, you may feel a kind of pseudo-love when the shutter clicks. That kind of feeling is more important than you think. The person being photographed is surprisingly sensitive to empty compliments (laugh).

I could almost hear Itami's voice saying,

"My wife is beautiful, isn't she!?"

You engage in multifaceted activities, similar to Director Itami.

No, no, that is not true. The fact that I have been able to work in various genres besides acting and modeling, such as illustrating, writing, and magazine editing, has all been made possible by good encounters and the good winds brought by the people around me. I don't have the vitality to create something from scratch. But I was always approached at the right time and asked, "Would you like to try something like this?" and always thought, "If there is something I can do, I would like to." It's the result of this kind of thing. I don't know why I am being urged to take on new things for no good reason, but I am still glad to have people ask me.

I heard you studied architecture in college.

That's why when I saw the shop's interior makeover at the movie's end, I wondered if Pisken had gone out of control. The Showa era worldview that had been consistent was suddenly modernized. The economic bubble must have led to that interior. Personally, I liked the original shop because it was tasteful, but it may be the ego of people today and urbanites to be too appreciative of the old things. When a shopping mall opens in their hometown, people in Tokyo irresponsibly get sentimental and say, "Oh, here we go again...," but the locals are happy nevertheless. Only time will tell what is appropriate and what is bad for each era and environment.

― 最後にお好きなサイドストーリーについて教えてください

母親になったこともあり、授乳シーンは出産時の自分と重ねて観てしまいました。もともと食が細めなのですが、食べなきゃ母乳も出ないので助産師さんにも心配されていました。実際長女が生まれてからはタガが外れたように米を食べるようになって、それが自分を介して子供に循環していくことを身をもって学びました。ホルモンバランスも関係して、授乳中に涙が止まらなくなることもありました。命を育てているっていう実感が、かつて経験したことのない感情を呼び起こした気がします。だから授乳シーンは自分にとって少し特別なのです。

evoked emotions

nurturing life

Realizing that I was
I had never experienced before.

Finally, please tell us about your favorite side story in the movie.

Having become a mother, I superimposed myself and the breastfeeding scene. My midwife was worried about me because I had always been a finicky eater, but if I didn't eat, I wouldn't be able to produce breast milk. In fact, after my first daughter was born, I went wild eating rice, and I learned firsthand that it circulates through me to my children. Sometimes I could not stop crying while breastfeeding, which had something to do with hormonal balance. Realizing that I was nurturing life evoked emotions I had never experienced before. So the breastfeeding scene is a little special to me.

命を育てているっていう実感が、かつて経験したことのない感情を呼び起こした気がします。

菊池亜希子（きくち・あきこ）
モデル／女優

多くの女性誌でモデルとして活躍する一方、その独特の存在感で女優としても注目され、映画『森崎書店の日々』(2010)で初主演を果たす。また、イラスト、エッセイなど活躍は多岐にわたる。自身が編集長を務めたライフスタイル・ファッションムック『菊池亜希子ムック マッシュ』（小学館）は累計56万部超えのヒットシリーズに。そして2児の母。

Akiko Kikuchi
Model / Actress

While working as a model for many women's magazines, Kikuchi also attracted attention as an actress with her unique presence and played her first leading role in the movie *The Days of Morisaki Bookstore* (Morisaki Shoten no Hibi; 2010). She also draws illustrations and writes essays. The lifestyle and fashion book *Akiko Kikuchi Mook Mash* (Shogakukan Inc.), for which she served as editor-in-chief, has become a hit series selling a cumulative total of over 560,000 copies. She is also the mother of two children.

【衣装協力】 unfil (03-5775-3383)　ORPHIC (alpha PR 03-5413-3546)

At a grocery store late at night

An old lady who is squeezing peaches and camembert

A wild goose chase like the Tom and Jerry show

Photograph_Yosuke Suzuki   Styling_Miwako Tanaka

○真夜中のスーパー

桃やカマンベールを押しつぶす老婦人
トムとジェリーさながらの追いかけっこ

10

執着心

An obsession

「触りたくて死にそう！」

中島敏子

若い頃、初めて伊丹十三を知り、憧れ、恐れ慄いたのが雑誌『mononcle』（モノンクル、ボクのおじさん）だった。

1981年に創刊され、わずか6号で休刊。しかし編集長である伊丹ほか〝おじさん〟たちの過剰な情熱は鮮烈な記憶として、後の私の編集者の基底でずっと蠢いていた。当時、生意気にも世の中の雑誌は皆なんだか軽佻浮薄だ！ 満足する雑誌がない！ とイキっていた自分には、クセの強いおじさま方の「精神世界の取り上げ方」が意味不明ながらたまらなく魅力だった。当時、大学の授業で福島章氏の「犯罪心理学」の講義も受けており、岸田秀氏の『ものぐさ精神分析』を愛読していたので、伊丹、福島、岸田というスタイリッシュな知性の組み合わせが作る『mononcle』は夢のような雑誌だった。

しかし今、手元に残っている1冊は、なぜかよりによって一番の問題作である4号目の「パリの人肉事件」特集なのである。これをうっかり見てしまい、伊丹十三を語る上でこの事件の犯人とされるサガワについて言及せずにはいられなくなってしまった。なんと100頁以上も使って、当時のフランスと日本の新聞記事のすべてを調べ上げてコピーで掲載、関係者のインタビュー、果ては大岡昇平、澁澤龍彦、加賀乙彦ら知の巨人たちの見解まで掲載している大特集だ。伊丹十三編集長の偏執さが本1冊まるごとに溢れ出ている。唾棄（だき）すべきエログロの最高潮に漂うインテリ

I Want to Touch so Bad I Could Die!

Toshiko Nakashima

When I was young, it was the magazine *mononcle* ("my uncle") through which I first heard of, admired, and was left shaken by Juzo Itami. The magazine appeared in 1981 and ceased publication after only six issues. However, vivid memories of the hyper-enthusiastic older "uncles" working under chief editor Itami were always bubbling under my own foundation as an editor later on. At the time, I had this attitude that there was always something frivolous about existing magazines. I proclaimed that "no magazine satisfies me." But there was something intensely appealing about these uncles with their strong peculiarities and their pieces on "how to deal with the spiritual world"—even if I didn't know what

that meant. At that point, I was taking Professor Akira Fukushima's lectures on criminal psychology and had carefully read Shu Kishida's "*Psychoanalysis for the Lazy*," so the stylish wisdom of Itami, Fukushima, and Kishida combining to create *mononcle* made it like a dream for me.

The only issue I have at hand now, for some odd reason, is the most problematic: the fourth issue featuring "The Case of the Paris Cannibal." When my eye fell on this, I could not help but mention Sagawa, the alleged perpetrator of this incident, when discussing Juzo Itami. It was a massive special issue of more than a hundred pages, with copy published after examination of every French and

ジェンス。そして2022年にイッセイサガワの訃報を聞いた時、思わずこの『mononcle』を思い出した。生と食と性と死と……これはあまりに『タンポポ』の各所に通底するテーマではないだろうか。

閑話休題。一度頭を冷やして、伊丹十三のスタイリッシュでフェティッシュで粘着質で観念的な、当初与えられたテーマを考えてみることにする。イカれたストーリー展開が矢継ぎ早に繰り広げられるこの映画の中でも、このシークエンスは異彩を放っている。

これは、いまどきの言葉で言えば「スーパーマーケットのクセツヨ老婆テロ」である。なぜ悪ノリした自意識過剰の食べ物テロは嫌悪されるのに、老婆のグロテスクな行為は映画のシークエンスとして成立するのか。触っちゃいけないものを触りたい、触感を自分の指で確かめたいという欲望は、本来誰の心の奥にもある。猫の肉球、犬の湿った鼻、赤ちゃんの頬、手、足、耳たぶ…。思わず手が出そうになるものが世の中には多過ぎる。

以前、私はファッション誌の編集長として頻繁にラグジュアリーブランドに触れていた。文字通り指で触れていた。高額な商品がずらーっと並んでいる展示会で、もちろん不躾に触ってはいけない。気をつけて注意深く軽く触るだけ。ふかふかのファー、艶めくベルベット、繊細なフェザー、ギラギラのラテックス…。もしかしたら、その時の私は今回の老婆のような目つきをしていたかもしれない。触感の欲望にギリギリのところで踏みとどまる理性があってよかった。高価な素材の素晴らしさは近くで見て(ちょっと触らないと)実感できない。こんな人が多いからか、特に高額で繊細で触りたくなる素材の洋服は、あらかじめビニールで覆われていた物も多かった。最適の犯罪防止である。

というわけで、状況に応じて人はギリギリのところで我慢する。おでんをツンツンする幼稚な行為とは異なり、これは成熟した大人のギリギリの衝動なのだ。ただ、その掟を破るとどうなるか。

深夜のスーパーマーケットで、店長(津川雅彦)が性格の悪そうな老婆(原泉)の"悪癖"を発見する。老婆は桃をむぎゅっと握る。桃の位置を変えては握り続ける。桃は初々しい若い女の肌のようだ。皺だらけの老婆がとうの昔に失ってしまった張りのある薄いピンクの肌、その弾力を指で確かめずにいられない。もみくちゃにしてやる。老婆の顔が歪む。まるで男が若

執着心

Japanese newspaper of the time and interviews of related persons. The issue even featured analyses by giants of the intellect like Shohei Ooka, Tatsuhiko Shibusawa, and Otohiko Kaga. The eccentric obstinacy of chief editor Juzo Itami overflowed to the extent that it would fill a whole book. It was intelligence floating at the despicable peak of *eroguro* "erotic grotesque". And then, when in 2022 I heard that Issei Sagawa had died, *mononcle* came to mind.

Life and food and sex and death...are these indeed not the themes underlying the various parts of *Tampopo*?

I will calm down for a while and try to consider the stylish, fetishistic, sticky, and theoretical Juzo Itami theme we were initially given. Even in the rapid-fire development of this maddening story, one sequence stands out.

In the words of today, this would be "the quirky granny's supermarket terrorism." Why does the old woman's grotesque act qualify as a film sequence when self-conscious food terrorism that got carried away is so hated? The desire to touch what you shouldn't touch, to see how something feels with your own hands, has always been deep in the hearts of us all. A cat's paw, a dog's moist nose, a baby's cheek, a hand, a foot, an earlobe; the world is just too full of things you want to reach out and touch.

I was frequently brought into contact with luxury brands as the chief editor of a fashion magazine. I literally fingered luxury goods. Of course, one cannot touch them impolitely when expensive products are lined up in a row. You touch lightly and very carefully. Fluffy fur, glossy velvet, delicate feathers, and glittering latex. It is possible that I had the same look in my eyes as that old lady, but fortunately, I had the good sense to stop before my tactile greed got the better of me. You only get a real sense of the magnificence of expensive materials by seeing them up close (and touching them a little). Perhaps many people are like this, so clothing, especially the expensive, delicate fabrics that make you want to touch it more, is largely covered beforehand in vinyl. The perfect crime prevention. So, depending on the situation, people go as far as they can and then stop. Unlike the childish act of stabbing at the various ingredients of oden to see what they are, a mature adult knows the limits to which their impulses should go. Although if these rules are broken, what happens then?

店長はハエ叩きで、ペシッと思い切り老婆の手を叩いて終了！　あくなき生への執着と食への執着。

ちなみに先のサガワは当時、川端康成に傾倒しており、その文章を緻密に分析している。日仏3名の識者とともに川端のさまざまな小説を語る鼎談記事の中で、『雪国』のエロティシズムについて侃侃諤諤の議論をしているのだが、彼は「指」と「会話」に着目して「こいつが一番よく君を覚えているよ」という部分が出てくるが、食べ物を指で押すという行為の禁忌は、もしかしたらマナーの問題よりエロティシズムの問題が奥に潜んでいるのかもしれない。あくなき食への執着と性への執着。そして死への狂気。

さて、現実社会に戻ろう。

2019年、こんなに触りたくてしょうがない私たちを、Covid-19は見事に引き離した。なぜCovid-19は私たちの大事な触覚をあそこまで奪ったのか。桃もチーズもパンも一切触れなくなった。触ることが罪になり、アクリルのパーテーションが私たちのすべてを極端に分断した。

い女をもみくちゃにするように老婆は桃をいたぶる。そこには「生」への執着がある。そして「性」への固執がある。最後にピュッと桃から出る汁はいかにもセクシュアルな暗喩だ。店長が気がついて追いかけ、老婆は逃げる。店長が先ほどの桃の具合を愛おしげに指でチェックすると、桃尻からツーッと汁が出る。

次に老婆はチーズ売り場でチーズの弾力を確かめている。少しハードめのものより、カマンベールチーズの弾力がお気に召したようだ。指を押し込みながら笑いを隠せない。「これよ、これ！」心の声が聞こえるようだ。そしてまたもや店長に見つかり、無音のまま追いかけっこ。チーズの棚に戻ってきた店長も指の跡が残るカマンベールにさらに自らの指を入れて弾力を確かめる。

トムとジェリーのような追いかけっこをしながら、老婆は片っ端から各種菓子パンをいじり倒す。それはもはや触感を楽しむというより餌を振り回しているハイエナだ。そうだ。これは夜のスーパーマーケットにおける"狩猟"なのだ。ハイエナとライオンという永遠の宿敵が命をかけた勝負。先行するハイエナは先に餌を見つけて食すが、追いかけてきたライオンである店長の本当の獲物はハイエナ、つまり老婆である。餌を振り回すハイエナを見つけて、ライオンの一撃！　餌べてを極端に分断した。

170　　　　執着心

The Manager (Masahiko Tsugawa) of the late-night supermarket discovers an unpleasant-looking old lady (Izumi Hara) indulging in a "bad habit." She squeezes a peach. Changing its position, she continues to grasp it as if it were the skin of an innocent young girl. The wrinkled old lady cannot resist confirming with her own hands the elasticity of the firm, light pink skin she lost long, long ago. This she will rub. Her face distorts. Just as a man rubs his hands over the body of a young girl, the old lady teases the peach. This is a fixation with "life." And a clinging to "sex." Certainly the juice that spurts from the peach at the end is a metaphor for sex. The manager notices and gives chase, and the old lady flees. Lovingly he checks the peach with his finger, and juice flows from it.

Next, the lady moves to the cheese section and checks the firmness of the product there. She prefers the softness of camembert more than the slightly harder cheeses. Pushing her finger into it, she cannot suppress a smile. It is as if we can hear her saying, "Yes! This is the one!" Now again, the manager sees her and silently gives chase. Returning to the cheese shelf, he also puts his finger into the camembert with the mark on it and checks its elasticity.

As this Tom and Jerry-like chase game goes on, the old lady fumbles with all the baked goods, knocking them over. Now, more than taking pleasure in the sense of touch, she is a hyena leaving a trail of food. That's right. Tonight in the supermarket, a hunt is in progress. A battle to the death between two traditional enemies, the hyena and the lion. The hyena, in the lead, finds and eats the food first, but the real prey of the pursuing lion, in the form of the store manager, is the hyena, in the form of the old lady. Finding the hyena throwing the food around, the lion strikes! With a fly swatter, the manager slaps the old lady's hand as hard as he can, and it's over! Obsession with life, obsession with food.

Incidentally, the aforementioned Sagawa was deeply into Yasunari Kawabata and closely analyzed his writing. In an article where he is one of three Japanese and French intellectuals discussing several Kawabata novels, there is a heated discussion of "eroticism" in *Snow Country*, during which he focuses on "fingers" and "conversation." Their discussion covers the section in which Shimamura, the central character, sticks out his index finger and says, "He's the guy who remembers you best." But the fact that sticking a finger into food is taboo may be more a question of deeply buried eroticism than

「何かに触れたい、触れる」という愉悦の時間を、機会を、場所を、取り上げられた。

快楽に浮かれるな、人類。

しかしそんな記憶も、もはや霧の中。私たちは今、少しずつ、物を触ったり人と触れたりしながら日常を取り戻そうとしている。しかしあの享楽に戻るのは怖いのだ。

一度、癌手術が成功した人も、その後も検査を余儀なくされることがあるように、未破裂動脈瘤がある人（私）が、必ず半年に一度検査しながら生き延びていくように、ここから先はいつ Covid が破裂するかもわからない。私のように「いつも隣にクモ膜下」を合言葉に元気に生きていくのがいいのではないだろうか。

笑止。

中島敏子（なかしま・としこ）
編集者

マガジンハウスに中途入社後、『BRUTUS』、『Tarzan』、『relax』副編集長などを経て 2011 年『GINZA』編集長に就任。2018 年独立、現在はフリーでプロデュース & 編集ほか。「Rakuten Fashion」にてエグゼクティブファッションクリエイティブディレクターも務める。

執着心

one of manners. Obsession with food, obsession with sex. And madness unto death.

To return to the present.

In 2019, we who so much wanted to touch were suddenly pulled apart by covid-19. Why did Covid-19 steal away so much of our precious sense of touch?

We couldn't touch peaches, cheese, or bread. Touching became a sin, and acrylic partitions divided us in ways we had never experienced before. The time, the chance, and the place for "wanting to be touched by something" and "wanting to touch something" was taken away.

Don't get carried away, humanity.

Memory is in a fog. Now, little by little, touching and being touched, we are getting back to our everyday lives. However, there is fear of returning to that pleasure.

In the same way that someone whose cancer operation has succeeded needs to be tested for the rest of their life, or someone like me with an unruptured brain aneurysm lives on while being tested every six months, Covid may break out again, so should the watchword by which we live not be "subarachnoid hemorrhage is always with us"? Absurd.

Translation_Ian MacDougall

Toshiko Nakashima
Editor

Nakashima joined Magazine House in mid-career and served as assistant chief editor for *BRUTUS*, *Tarzan*, and *Relax* before being appointed chief editor of *GINZA* in 2011. She went independent in 2018 and now works, among other things, as a freelance producer and editor. She is the executive fashion creative director for "Rakuten Fashion."

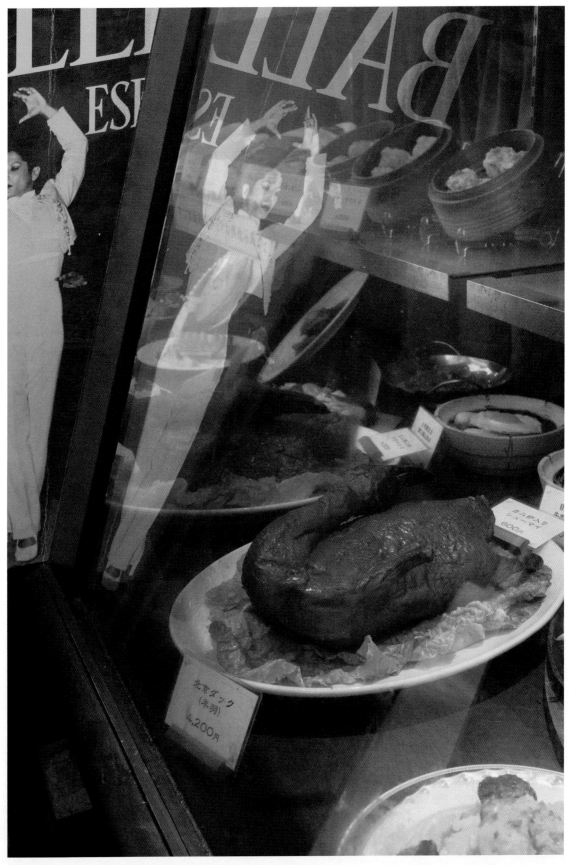

北京ダック
（半羽）
4,200円

174

Photograph_Robert Baka

「ダンナぁ、お願いです」

「すみませんが、行く前に、

Words of Outsiders

11

A little white lie

愛すべき嘘

Do me a favor.

Please, before we go...   just one more.

ひとつだけ」

美食の都・サンセバスチャンで"タンポポ"を観た。

杉山恒太郎

この秋3年ぶりにヨーロッパの途に。向かったのはスペイン・サンセバスチャンの街、バスク有数の美景の古都であり今や世界のフーディ（foodie）たち垂涎の美食の街でもある。僕も考えたら今回で3度目となる。立ち飲みバルが100軒は下らないと言われる旧市街でのバルホッピング（バルのはしご、だ）はなんとも魅惑的で癖になるのだ。

ここで開かれる映画祭はカンヌ、ベニス、ベルリンに次いで今や欧州4大映画祭の1つと称されるほどの盛況ぶり。その発展を支えてきた要因の1つはここの「食」にあるのは間違いない。僕たちだって京都だ金沢だ沖縄だ、と言われれば目的はともあれまずは「美味しいものに有りつけそう！」感が脳裡を駆け巡るだろう。そんな背景をもつサンセバスチャン国際映画祭での2022年日本からの招待映画はなんとあの伊丹十三の"タンポポ"だと聞いて胸が高鳴った。ずいぶんとご無沙汰ではあるこの映画、今この時代、この時期、海外のこの地で観たらどんな印象を僕に残してくれるのだろうか。興味は尽きない。ましてや今の日本の薄っぺらなグルメブームを先読みしていたかのような「食の映画／タンポポ」。その"にわか食通たち"への監督・伊丹十三による洗練された風刺と知的でシニカルな笑いは海外の人々に一体どう映るのだろうか。僕も冒頭でfoodieと敢えて記したのは今声高に叫ばれる"グルメ"という言葉がむずついて仕方なく、ジョークとして遣うならとも

　　　　愛すべき嘘

Tampopo in San Sebastian, the World's Food Capital

Kotaro Sugiyama

This fall, I set out for Europe for the first time in three years. My destination was the city of San Sebastian in Spain, an ancient town with some of the most beautiful scenery in the Basque country, which today sets watering the mouths of foodies from all over the world. Now that I have mentioned it, this was my third visit. They say there are well over 100 "stand-up" bars in the old town, and bar-hopping there is both delightful and addictive. The film festival held here is so successful that it is now considered one of Europe's four major such gatherings, after Cannes, Venice, and Berlin. It is certainly true that "food" is one of the factors that has sustained the festival. Whatever our purpose in

going somewhere, whether it be Kyoto or Kanazawa or Okinawa, the first thing that comes to mind is, "there'll be something delicious to eat there!" With that in the back of my mind, my heart beat faster when I heard that none other than Juzo Itami's famous *Tampopo* had been invited to the 2022 San Sebastian International Film Festival. After so many years, what impression would this movie leave on me in this era, these times, in a foreign land? My curiosity had no end, especially as *Tampopo*, this movie of food, has foreseen the rather shallow gourmet boom currently happening in Japan. How would director Juzo Itami's cynical laughter at these "fair-weather gourmets," with its mix of fine sarcasm and wisdom, play out with

かく真っ直ぐに遭う勇気など持ち合わせてはないのために奮闘するという一見みなれた痛快活劇だ。さ、てさて次に何が起こるのか？　満員の観客は固唾をのなぁ（w）。

んでスクリーンを覗いていたのだが、そっから！　が大変なことになる（w）。突然、いや、唐突に脈絡なくエロく濃い13のエピソードが飛び込んでくるのだ。

さてパリ経由ビルバオで一泊、翌朝ゲタリアの〝ELKANO／エルカノ〟で仲間たちと昼食を。世界広しといえどもこんなに魚に精通した料理屋を他には知らない。それは眼前にカンタブリア海という世界有数の漁場にも恵まれた所以なのか。アルバリーニョの白ワインとともに名物料理〝ココチャ／バスク語kokotxa、スペイン語／cococha〟を注文。これはな、にかといえば〝魚の喉肉〟、小指の先程の小さな部位だがそれは美味を超え禁断の味わい（w）。そして今夜はサンセバ（僕たち日本人は何でも省略したがるw）、明日午後はいよいよ〝タンポポ〟の上映、チケットは既にソウルドアウト、満席だと聞いて自分のことのように嬉しくもあり何故かほっと安堵したのだった。そして満を持してバスク初公開、ジャパニーズ・ラーメン・ウエスタン（らーめん西部劇）〝タンポポ〟の上映が始まった。女手ひとつで寂れたラーメン屋を営む美しい未亡人（宮本信子）と、彼女に惹かれるタンクローリー車の運転手（山崎努）が、流浪（さすらい）のガンマンよろしくカウンター越しに難癖をつけにやって来るチンピラたちを蹴散らしラーメン屋再興

生卵を口移しに互いの盛りを亢進し合うギャング（役所広司）と愛人、公園の闇の奥、焚き火を囲むホームレスたちの怪しい美食パーティー、また年老いた詐欺師（中村伸郎）が尾行してきた刑事（田武謙三）に逮捕、手錠を掛けられても尚も手にした烤鴨餅（カォヤーピン）で挟み北京ダックを貪る、その恍惚とした表情に潜む人の強欲さは他人事ではない。

「今まで文学や映画でも、色気についてはいろいろ描かれてきましたが、食い気についてはあまり扱われてきませんでしたね。〝タンポポ〟は、そういう点で、〝食い気〟の中の、ユーモア、厳粛さ、ブラックユーモア、そして狂気まで追求した映画だと思いますね」と中村伸郎はあるインタビューでこう答えているがまさに言い得て妙。

さて僕のまわりに座った観客たちはといえば息をひそめ戸惑いを隠さず、これを果して〝笑っていいも、

people from outside Japan? I deliberately used the word "foodie" at the beginning of this because I can't help being irritated with people shouting "gourmet," a word which, even if I were to use it as a joke, I still do not dare to proclaim myself with a straight face (laugh).

Anyway, via Paris to Bilbao for one night, then to the Restaurante Elkano in Getaria for lunch with friends the following day. In the whole wide world, no other restaurant knows its fish this well. Could this be because they are blessed with the Cantabrian Sea, one of the world's best fishing grounds, right before their eyes? With Albariño white wine, we order their most famous dish kokotxa, in Basque, or cococha, in Spanish. This is the fleshy part of the fish jaw, a small piece about the size of the tip of a little finger, but a taste so far past "good" that it should be forbidden. And then tonight it's "Sanseba" (as we in Japan like to abbreviate "San Sebastian" like we abbreviate everything else) and the screening of *Tampopo* coming up tomorrow afternoon. I was as delighted to hear that the tickets were already sold out and the house would be full as I would be if the movie were my own, but I was also relieved for some reason. And now comes the long-awaited Basque-country premier, and the screening begins of this "Japanese ramen western," *Tampopo*. In this seemingly familiar thrilling action movie, a lone gunman in the form of a tank-truck driver (Tsutomu Yamazaki) wanders into town and, fascinated with a beautiful widow (Nobuko Miyamoto) trying to run a failing ramen restaurant alone, fights to revive the establishment by driving away a gang of thugs who swarm over the counter to cause trouble. And so...now what happens? The sold-out audience watches with bated breath, and then! Something incredible happens. Suddenly, out of the blue, with no logical connection among them, come flying thirteen darkly erotic episodes. Among them are that of the gangster (Koji Yakusho) and his moll, their mutual excitement rising as they transfer the raw egg from mouth to mouth; the weird gourmet party of the homeless around a bonfire deep in a park; and the elderly con man (Nobuo Nakamura) arrested by the detective (Kenzo Tabu) who has been trailing him, and who, even though his hands are cuffed, still craves the pancake-wrapped Peking duck. The greed that lurks beneath the expression of ecstasy on their faces is something we can all understand.

Nobuo Nakamura, in an interview, summed it up perfectly. "Desire has been portrayed in different ways in books and movies, but gluttony has not," he said. "*Tampopo*, in that sense, is a movie which

のか否か〟 そんな気配りが辺りを支配し、鼈（すっぽん）をシメ鮮血が飛び散るシーンでは悲鳴まで轟いた。これがニューヨークやパリなら各エピソードに観客はドッと沸き大笑いすると訊いたんだけど（※実は、海外での評価は驚くべきもので、シネフィルお馴染みのRotten Tomatoesでは2021年現在、100%フレッシュ獲得！ 食欲と魂の栄養という普遍的なテーマを描ききった傑作コメディと未だに高評価、1987年全米公開、同年の米国公開の外国映画で5位にランクイン、興収400万ドルの大ヒットであった）。待てよ、こうしてみるとバスクの人たちは確かにお行儀のよい人が多いけれど、だからこそ僕の前ではどっと映笑（こうしょう）しなかっただけできっと映画館の帰り路、あの旧市街で各々が馴染みの立ち呑みバルに飛び込みチャコリ（微発泡白ワイン）をグラスにPintxos／ピンチョス（バスクではTapasと言わない）で舌鼓、あの得も言われぬ〝試写会の空気感〟から全面開放！ さぞかしシュールな各エピソードを酒肴に〝思い出しては笑い転げている〟ことは想像に難くない。そう気付き、僕の杞憂も彼方に消え去った（w）。

さてこの映画の構成のお手本となったのがルイス・ブニュエルの「自由の幻想」だったということは伊丹マニアによく知られていること。ブニュエルといえばダリとの共作「アンダルシアの犬」から始まり「黄金時代」など筋金入りのシュールレアリスト、と同時にそんな肩書では収まらない僕の20代の頃私淑していた映画のメンター（Mentor）だ。映画「悲しみのトリスターナ」出演のためパリから飛んできたカトリーヌ・ドヌーヴを、ブニュエルは彼女に履かせるための義足を大事そうに抱え、微笑みを浮かべて飛行場にまでわざわざ迎えに来たという、仰天の逸話を残す稀代の巨匠でもあるのだ。そういえば自由の幻想の前作「ブルジョワジーの秘かな愉しみ」も〝食事しようとする人が奇妙な出来事のため食事にありつけない〟食にまつわる謎だらけの贅沢な映画だった。

「やっぱり映画って、いろんな映画に対するオマージュで成り立っていると思うんですよね」伊丹十三の妻にして伊丹映画のミューズ、宮本信子の言葉。〝映画を観る〟ってその一本だけを観るのではなくって自分のそれまでの映画的記憶をかきあつめて愉しむものだと僕も思う。

さてここまで来てあらためて戴いた依頼書をながめたらあの北京ダックと老詐欺師のエピソードをもとに

sought the humor, the harsh truth, the black humor, and even the craziness in a person's appetite."

The people sitting around me, watching with bated breath, could not hide their uncertainty, and sure enough, there was a feeling of "should we laugh at this or not." Screams were heard during the scene in which fresh turtle blood sprays around. I've heard that audiences in places like New York and Paris laughed loudly at these episodes. In fact, reaction to the film abroad was a surprise, with the Rotten Tomatoes site, familiar to cinephiles, rating it "100% Fresh" on its "Tomatometer" in 2021. Even now, it is rated as a comedy masterpiece for portraying the universal theme of appetite and nourishment of the soul. When it opened across the U.S. in 1987, it ranked fifth among foreign movies released that year, a huge hit with $4 million in box office receipts. But wait; seen this way, most of the people of the Basque country do appear to be reserved and well-mannered, so of course they wouldn't even giggle in front of me, but it was not hard to imagine how, after they left, they would pile into those good old stand-up bars in the old town, savor a glass of white Txakoli wine, and snack on pintxos (the Basques don't call them "tapas".) Freed from that unique atmosphere of a movie screening, they would surely roll around

laughing, making a meal of each surreal episode. Realizing this made my worries vanish into thin air.

Every Itami maniac knows very well that the model for the structure of this movie was Luis Buñuel's *The Phantom of Liberty*. With Buñuel, we start with *An Andalusian Dog*, made together with Salvador Dalí, and such hardcore surrealism as *The Golden Age*, but that description fails to cover a figure who was, for me in my 20s, a movie mentor. He was a rare maestro about whom are told astonishing stories. He is said to have gone to the airport to meet Catherine Deneuve, flying in from Paris to star in his movie *Tristiana*, smiling and carefully holding the prosthetic leg she was to wear in her role. Now that I mention this, the Buñuel work that precedes *The Phantom of Liberty*, *The Discreet Charm of the Bourgeoisie*, is also a film of luxurious excess full of food-related mysteries, where strange events prevent a group of diners from actually having a meal.

"I think a movie is put together out of homages to a lot of other movies," says Nobuko Miyamoto, the wife of Juzo Itami and the muse for his films. I agree that watching a movie is not just seeing one film but gathering your memories of all the movies you have ever seen.

"愛すべき嘘"をテーマに言及することが僕の役目だったことを再確認する。詐欺師の奥義に「疑い深い人間ほど騙しやすい！」というのを訊いたことがある。またピカソは「こどもの嘘は、クリエーティブの目覚め」と言った。また近松門左衛門は「芸というものは実と虚の皮膜（ひにく）の間にあるもの他」と。この芸をそのまま映画という言葉に置き換えてみると"タンポポ"の様々な"愛すべき悪戯（いたずら）"の仕掛けが読めてくる。そこで気がかりなことがある。果して今の僕たちにはそんな嘘を心から愉しめる心の遊びと酔狂さと器量を持ち合わせているのだろうか。この半世紀、「伊丹十三の不在」はあまりにも痛い。

杉山恒太郎（すぎやま・こうたろう）
株式会社ライトパブリシティ 代表取締役社長

大学卒業後、電通入社。1990年代後半よりデジタル領域のリーダーとしてインタラクティブ・コミュニケーションの確立に貢献。トラディショナル広告とデジタル広告の両方を熟知した数少ないエグゼクティブ クリエイティブディレクター。

Having come this far and having another look at the request I received for this piece, I remember that my role was to reference the theme of the "lovable lie" based on the Peking duck and elderly con man episode. I have heard that a con man's secret is that "the most suspicious are the easiest to deceive." Picasso also said that "a child's lies are a creative awakening." Also, "art is between the membrane of the real and the lie," says the medieval playwright Chikamatsu Monzaemon. Exchanging the word "art" for "film" makes it possible for us to see the mechanisms of *Tampopo*'s various "lovable mischiefs." But therein lies a worry. Do we have the playfulness, eccentricity, and talent today to truly enjoy such lies? Over the past half-century, the absence of Juzo Itami has been too painful.

Translation_Ian MacDougall

Kotaro Sugiyama
President Light Publicity Co., Ltd.

Sugiyama joined Dentsu Inc. following graduation from university. In the late 1990s, as a leader in the digital field, he contributed to the establishment of interactive communications. He is among the few executive creative directors knowledgeable in both traditional and digital advertising.

THERE WAS A TIME

Photographs by Parker Fitzgerald

ネットフリックスの人気シリーズ『シェフのテーブル』でアイバン・オーキンのことを知ったときの衝撃を、なんと言い表すべきだろう。ジャズはスイングするのが当たり前と思っていた時代にチャーリー・パーカーのビバップで面食らうような、そんな強い衝撃を受けたし、実際彼はその映像の中で疾走するジャズをBGMに、捲し立てるように己の人生を語る。料理の道を志すまでもがき苦しみ、日本を愛して身を浸し、一流のラーメン職人として名を馳せてニューヨークに凱旋するサクセスストーリーだけでも十分だったのに、彼が『タンポポ』のファンであることを知ったならインタビューを申し込まないわけにはいかなかった。

どうして『タンポポ』で描かれるラーメンがあれほど美味しく見えてくるのか？　その理由のひとつは、これがどんぶりから溢れるように食べること・生きること・死ぬことを伝えるドラマであればこそ。だから、その生き方が圧倒的に魅力溢れるアイバン・オーキンのラーメンもまた、当然絶品なのだ。

ジューイッシュのルーツと東京で築いたキャリアをひとつのアートフォームに昇華したアイバン・オーキンが教えてくれる、人生のマル秘レシピをとくとご覧あれ！

アイバン・オーキン

Ivan Orkin

How can I describe the shock I felt when I learned about Ivan Orkin from the popular Netflix series *Chef's Table*? The impact it had on me was quite strong, like encountering Charlie Parker's bebop when I took it for granted that jazz music was supposed to swing. In fact, in that show, Orkin goes on and on about his life story as jazz hurtles forward in the background. Orkin's success story-his struggle to pursue a culinary career, his love for and immersing himself in Japan, and his triumphant return to New York City after making a name for himself as a first-rate ramen chef-alone was enough, but once I learned that he was a fan of *Tampopo*, I just had to request an interview.

Why does the ramen depicted in *Tampopo* look so delicious? One reason is that it's a drama about eating, living, and dying, just like ramen overflows from its bowl. So, naturally, the ramen of Orkin, whose way of living overflows with appealing qualities, is also excellent.

Here, Ivan Orkin, who brought his Jewish roots and Tokyo career up to the level of art, shares his secret recipe for life with us, so enjoy!

Voices of Outsiders 　　 5

Interview_Makoto Miura (COLAXO)
Photographs_Kohei Kawashima
Translation_Akemi Nakamura (Interview), Trivector Co., Ltd. (Article)

だから『タンポポ』を観れば観るほど、日本のことを知ることもできた。

So the more I watched *Tampopo*, the more I learned about Japan.

―『タンポポ』をはじめて観たのは？

1985年か86年で、コロラド大学にいたときだったね。日本語を学びたくて大学を探したら、コロラド大学に日本語の専攻学科があった。つまり高校生の時点で日本に興味があったわけだけど、それは1978年に友達に誘われて寿司レストランでバイトしていたから。スタッフはみんな日本人。僕はいつも腹ペコで、シェフたちはとても親切だったのでよくご飯を食べさせてもらった。寿司はもちろん、いかの塩辛のような珍味までね。この経験が日本への興味へと繋がった。当時日本食のレストランはコロラドにも生まれ故郷のニューヨークにもまだ少なかったと思う。食べることは大好きだったけど、まだラーメンについてはなにも知らなかった。だから『タンポポ』を観てラーメンのことを知ったんだ。

―『タンポポ』で最初に抱いた感想は？

最初はあまり理解できなかった。でもそれから40回以上は観ていると思う。大学を出てからも日本語や日本の文化について学び、実際に日本に住み、日本人の妻を迎え、働いた。日本を知るほどに『タンポポ』の何が面白くて、何が悲しいのかを理解できるようになった。だから『タンポポ』を観れば観るほど、日本のことを知ることもできた。例えばスパゲティ講座のシーン。奥さんのおかげでその面白さを理解することができたけど、西洋と日本における麺の食べ方が異なることを前提としながら、ルールに従うはずの日本人が揃ってがさつな外国人の真似をしてスパッゲティを食べることになる。正解と不正解が混在している点が魅力的だと思う。

When did you first see Tampopo?

It was 1985 or 86 when I was at the University of Colorado. I was looking for a college to study Japanese and found that the University of Colorado had a major in it. In other words, I was already interested in Japan as a high school student. This was because my friend had invited me to work part-time at a sushi restaurant in 1978. All the staff was Japanese. I was always hungry, and the chefs were really kind, so they fed me well. Sushi, of course, and even delicacies such as the squid dish ika no shiokara. This experience led to my interest in Japan. At the time, there weren't many Japanese restaurants in Colorado or my hometown, New York City. I loved eating, but I still didn't know anything about ramen. So, I learned about ramen after watching *Tampopo*.

What was your first impression of Tampopo?

At first, I didn't understand much. But I think I've seen it over 40 times since then. After college, I continued learning about the Japanese language and culture, lived in Japan, married a Japanese woman, and worked. The more I learned about Japan, the more I understood what was interesting and sad in *Tampopo*. So the more I watched *Tampopo*, the more I learned about Japan. For example, the scene of the spaghetti class. Thanks to my wife, I could understand what was funny about it. The way of eating noodles in the West and Japan are different, and the Japanese—the rule-followers—all eat spaghetti in a way that imitates the rude foreigner. I find the mixture of correctness and incorrectness appealing.

—— ほかに印象的なシーンは？

一番好きなのはサラリーマンたちがホテルで会食するシーン。年老いた重役たちが明らか
に若い社員を見下している中で、彼が一番洗練されていて、料理について熟知していて、
そこで何を注文すべきか心得ていた。結果的にその場にいる全員を打ち負かしてしまう。
伊丹十三の映画の魅力は日本人のさまざまな感情の、機微の変化を描いているところで、
その日本固有の風習を少しからかうような視点もある。それこそが彼が映画作家として優
れていた点で、日本人がはっきりと言えないようなことに着目して、それを賢い方法で映
画に落とし込んでいた。でも外国人である僕が日本に暮らしながら、日本固有の風習をか
らかうようなことはできなかったね。もちろん日本に対するリスペクトがあったし、なに
よりとても親切にしてもらっていたから。

—— 日本ではどんな方々がサポートしてくれましたか？

まずは香川にある大和製作所の社長さん。ラーメン博で会い、彼の会社の製麺機を購入し
て家でラーメンの作り方を研究した。スープもオリジナルで完璧なものを追い求め、鶏ガ
ラスープに魚介エキスを加えた塩ベースのダブルスープに辿り着いた。味見は常に奥さん
がしてくれた。彼女が美味しいと言ってくれるまで試作を繰り返したよ。それに彼女の兄
は大工だったから、ついに世田谷の芦花公園に「アイバンラーメン」をオープンするとき
は、ピスケンのように手伝ってくれたよ。お店は 1980 年代からあるような商店街にあっ
たから、個人経営の肉屋さんや魚屋さん、それに八百屋さんもみんながやさしく助けてく
れた。ラーメンを作るための素材は常に近隣で手にすることができた。

日本人がはっきりと言えないようなことに**着目**して、それを**賢い方法**で映画に落とし込んでいた。

He **focused on** things that the Japanese could not say clearly and put them into a film in **a clever way.**

What other scenes were memorable?

My favorite scene is when the businessmen are having dinner at a hotel. The older executives are clearly looking down on the younger employee, but he was the most sophisticated and knowledgeable about the food and knew what to order. As a result, he beats everyone else in the room. The appeal of Juzo Itami's films lies in the way he depicts the various emotions and subtleties of the Japanese people, with a viewpoint that pokes a bit of fun at their unique customs. That is what made him so good as a filmmaker: he focused on things that the Japanese could not say clearly and put them into a film in a clever way. But as a foreigner living in Japan, I could not make fun of the unique Japanese customs. Of course, I had respect for Japan, and above all, they were very kind to me.

What kind of people supported you in Japan?

First, the president of Yamato Manufacturing in Kagawa. I met him at a Ramen expo and bought his company's noodle-making machine to study how to make ramen at home. I also wanted to make an original and perfect soup and arrived at a salt-based double broth with chicken soup and seafood extract. My wife always did the tasting. I tried it over and over again until she said it was delicious. And her brother was a carpenter, so when I finally opened Ivan Ramen in Roka Koen, Setagaya, he helped me, like Pisuken. The shop was in a shopping district that had been there since the 1980s, so the independent butcher, fishmonger, and greengrocer were all kind enough to help us out. The ingredients for making ramen were always available in the neighborhood.

I believed in my science

しきたりよりも、自分の**サイエンス**を信じて、形にすることができたんだ。

— 日本で大変だったことは？

2007年にお店をオープンさせるまではとても長い道のりだったし、決して楽ではなかった。最初に日本に降り立ったのは1987年で、渋谷のベルリッツで英語の講師をしていた。実は生徒に宮本信子さんがいて、息子である池内万平さん、万作さんにも毎週教えていたよ。ラーメンを好きになってはいたけど、まだ作る決心には至っていなかった。むしろ人生に悩み、3年でまたアメリカに戻り、そこから10年以上ラーメンとは無縁の暮らし。アメリカで食べようとは思えなかった。レストラン業界で経験を積んだのち、日本に戻り、空前のラーメンブームを目の当たりにした。そして妻に東京で最高のラーメン屋になること宣言した。しかも独学でね。すでにシェフとしての経験はあったけれど、ラーメンに関してはなにが正しくて、なにが悪いのかもわからない。ましてや日本人は「こうしなければいけない！」っていう思いが強いから。だから自分はあえて外国人の視点のまま作っていこうと思った。しきたりよりも、自分のサイエンスを信じて、形にすることができたんだ。

more than convention, and I was able to make it a reality.

What were some of the challenges you faced in Japan?

It was a very long road to open the store in 2007. It certainly wasn't easy. I first landed in Japan in 1987, teaching English at Berlitz in Shibuya. One of my students was actually Nobuko Miyamoto, and I also taught her sons Manpei and Mansaku Ikeuchi every week. I had fallen in love with ramen but had not yet made up my mind to make it. Not sure what to do with my life, I returned to the U.S. after three years and then lived without ramen for more than ten years. I could not bring myself to eat ramen in the U.S. After gaining experience in the restaurant industry, I returned to Japan and witnessed the unprecedented ramen boom. I then declared to my wife that I would start the best ramen place in Tokyo—self-taught. I already had experience as a chef, but I didn't know what was good and bad when it came to ramen. And Japanese people strongly feel that one has to do things a certain way. That's why I ventured to make it from a foreigner's point of view. I believed in my science more than convention, and I was able to make it a reality.

── アメリカに戻ろうと思った理由を教えてください

父が高齢になったことや、2011年の東日本大震災で売上が半分になってしまったうえ、計画停電で仕事をしたくてもできない状態になった。震災がなければ日本で死んでもいいと思えるくらい日本のことが好きだったのに。しかもアメリカで開業するために、日本でやっていたさまざまなことを変えなければいけなかった。日本の小麦を使うとどうしても高くなってしまうからカナダ産に切り替えることにしたり、高い家賃をカバーするためにはメニューも増やさないといけなかった。アメリカ人は選択肢を求めてくるしね。

── 今、一番のおすすめは？

提供するメニュー以上に気にしていることがあって、お客さんにもっと日本のことを知ってもらいたいって思っているし、日本がなぜ特別な国なのかっていうことを教えたいんだ。レストランを経営することは食べ物を作ることだけじゃない。もしかしたら食べ物を作ることが一番簡単なのかもしれない。そしてこの店に来たら、来る前よりも幸せになって帰ってもらいたい。そんな様子は、『タンポポ』でも描かれていたことだと思う。お店に居たら、遠くからだって不幸せな顔をしている人はすぐわかる。僕はその見極めが得意なんだ。そんな思いを胸に頑張って、世界中にお店を持てたら最高だよね。

Why did you decide to return to the U.S.?

My father was getting old, and in addition to the Great East Japan Earthquake in 2011 cutting our sales in half, the rolling blackouts made it impossible for me to work even if I wanted to. I loved Japan so much that I would have been willing to die in Japan if not for the earthquake. Moreover, to open a shop in the U.S., I had to change many things I had been doing in Japan. Using Japanese wheat would inevitably be more expensive, so we had to switch to Canadian wheat, and we also had to increase our menu choices to cover the higher rent. And Americans wanted choices.

Currently what's your recommended dish?

There are things I care about more than what we serve. I want my customers to know more about Japan and why Japan is a special country. Running a restaurant is more than just making food. Perhaps making food is the easiest part. And when they come to this restaurant, I want them to leave happier than before. I believe *Tampopo* also depicted this kind of thing. In the shop, I can easily spot someone with an unhappy face, even from a distance. I'm good at discerning that kind of thing. It would be great if I could work hard with that mindset and have shops worldwide.

アイバン・オーキン

コロラド大学在学中にラーメンの虜になり、日本に在住。アメリカに戻り、The Culinary Institute of America NY を卒業後、有名店で働くが、ラーメンを求めて再来日。2007 年、東京・世田谷に「アイバンラーメン」をオープンするも、2011 年の東日本大震災後アメリカに帰国。ニューヨークのロウアー・イースト・サイドに拠点を移し、ネットフリックスの『シェフのテーブル』で特集され、注目の的となる。

Ivan Orkin

While attending the University of Colorado, Ivan became captivated by ramen and moved to Japan. After returning to the U.S. and graduating from the Culinary Institute of America NY, he worked at famous restaurants but went back to Japan in search of ramen. In 2007, he opened Ivan Ramen in Setagaya, Tokyo, but again returned to the U.S. after the Great East Japan Earthquake in 2011. Relocating his business to New York City's Lower East Side, he became the center of attention when featured on Netflix's *Chef's Table*.

食べること
生きること

TO EAT　　TO LIVE

　Photograph_Tetsuya Ito

Words of Outsiders

12

「おまえら食え」

「かあちゃんがつくった最期のご飯だ。

今ならまだあったかい。

食べろ、

おい、食うんだ」

Keep eating!

It's the last meal your mother cooked!

Eat while it's hot!　　**Eat!**

「最期の晩餐」

平松洋子

世間に、「最期の晩餐には何を食べたいですか」という問いがある。しかし、自分がどんな「最期」を迎えることになるのか、誰にも予測はつかず、自分でシナリオを描けるわけではなく、そのとき何かを食べられる状態かどうかもわからない。そもそも、自分の「最期」を想定すること自体がファンタジーの領域だろう。なのに、私たちはこの問いを手放さず、一個人の核心を突くフレーズであるかのように扱ったりもする。いや、本当は、リアルな現実から逃避するための言葉遊びなのかもしれないけれど。

『タンポポ』に登場する「白服の男」の最期は、じつに含蓄に富んでいる。どしゃぶりの雨に打たれながら、銃弾に倒れた男が今際のきわにつぶやくのは、狩ったイノシシを捌いてすぐさま取り出した腸への偏愛。山芋がぎっしり詰まった腸詰はめっぽううまいらしい、と夢想しながら切れ切れに語り、それを聞く情婦は「そうね、わさび醤油なんか合うわね」。語り終えた男は、あたかも味わったあとの満足気な笑みを浮かべ、そのまま絶命する。彼は、まさか自分の「最期の晩餐」がイノシシの腸詰の夢想だなんて思いもかけなかったはずだ。情婦や少女との食をめぐる官能的な悦びにさんざん溺れてきたのに、「最期の晩餐」は伝聞や想像の産物だった——伊丹十三そのひとのシニシズムに触れて背筋がぞくりとするのだが、いや待てよ、と思う。手

The Last Supper

Yoko Hiramatsu

People sometimes ask each other, "What would you like to have for your last supper?" However, nobody can predict what kind of "last" they will face, and no one knows what condition they will be in when it comes time to eat that final something. And anyway, even imagining your "last" puts you in the realm of fantasy. Nonetheless, we do not abandon this question, using it as if it were a phrase by which we could break through to a person's heart. In fact, though, it may simply be a word game by which we can escape reality.

The death of the man in the white suit who appears in *Tampopo* is, in fact, rich in significance. In the pouring rain, shot down and on the verge of death, he murmurs of his taste for intestines prepared from a freshly hunted wild boar. Sausages stuffed tightly with yam are very, very good, he says in faltering tones as he drifts in and out of a dream state, upon hearing which his moll responds, "Yes...Perfect with soy sauce and wasabi." The man has stopped speaking, a satisfied smile as though he had just savored the dish comes to his face, and he breathes his last. Never in his wildest dreams would he have thought his "last supper" would be a wild-boar sausage. Even as he has wallowed in the sensual pleasure of food with his moll or the young girl, this "last supper" is a product of hearsay or imagination.

の届かない未知の味ほどロマンなものはな
いのだから、白服の男は伊丹監督によって悦楽の極み
を与えられたともいえる──。

『タンポポ』には、生と死のイメージが全編に横溢
している。ラーメン・ウェスタンは世を忍ぶ仮の姿。
エンタテインメントの衣を着せつつ官能に迫る映画を
撮りたいという伊丹十三の欲望を強烈に感じる一作
だ。それまで折に触れて書いてきた食べものと官能性
にまつわる文章を映像化する試みでもあっただろう。
だから、ルイス・ブニュエルを多分に意識したシュー
ルな映像表現を取り入れもした。かくして、重層的に
響き合うエピソードの連続とイメージの集積が『タン
ポポ』を唯一無二の映画にすることになった。

「走る男」にも驚かされる。わずか三分三十秒ほど
のシークエンスだが、彼岸と此岸を結び合わせる傑作
だ。じっさい、このワンシーンが挟み込まれなければ、
『タンポポ』の作品世界の深みはずいぶん違うものに
なっただろう。観る者の経験、立場、考え方などによっ
て受けとる深度も角度も異なる、いわば普遍性を帯び
た三分三十秒だ。

夫は、瀕死の妻を現世に引き留めようとして叫ぶ。
「そうだ、飯をつくれ。かあちゃん、晩飯の支度だ」
とっさに台所を指差すと、妻はふわあと起き上がり、
台所に立ってねぎを刻み、こしらえた炒飯を「できた
よ」と、中華鍋ごとちゃぶ台に運ぶ。間髪入れず自分
の茶碗によそう夫と三人の幼子の姿を見届ける母の微
笑は、慈母のそれ。次の瞬間、畳の上に倒れ込み、天
命をまっとうして旅立った妻のかたわらで、父は子ら
に叫ぶ。

「おまえら食え。かあちゃんがつくった最期のご飯
だ。今ならまだあったかい。食べろ、おい、食うんだ」
生きとし生けるものの究極の関係が描き尽される場
面である。授かった子らを、自分の命を賭して守ろ
とする親。むき出しの本能を、母性を、一食の炒飯を
通して描き出す伊丹十三の洞察と才気に圧倒される。
鬼気迫る異様な情景なのに、なにか浄化されたような
清らかさがスクリーンから立ち上ってくる。

『タンポポ』が公開された一九八五年、世相はきわめ
て激しく揺れ動いていた。「科学万博 つくば・85」が
開催され、男女雇用機会均等法が成立、阪神が二十一
年ぶりにセ・リーグ優勝、ラーメンブームが生まれ、

The cynicism of Juzo Itami sends chills down my spine, but then I think, "Wait." Nothing conjures romance so much as an unknown, unachievable taste, so through the director, the man in white may have scaled the heights of pleasure.

Tampopo overflows with images of life and death. "Ramen western" is a disguise under which it hides. It is a work that makes one feel strongly Juzo Itami's urge to make an arousing film in the guise of popular entertainment. He probably also wanted to try making a film out of the writing he did from time to time, linking food and sensuality. That is why he incorporated surrealist imagery heavily influenced by Luis Buñuel. This series of episodes reverberating in multiple layers with each other and its accumulation of images make *Tampopo* a film like no other.

The "Running Man" also surprises. The sequence, only about three minutes and 30 seconds long, is a masterpiece linking this world and the next. In fact, had this scene not been inserted, the film world of *Tampopo* would have had a very different depth. This three minutes and 30 seconds have a universality that people will interpret at different depths and angles, depending on such factors as their experiences, standpoints, and ways of thinking.

"I've got it!" shouts the husband, trying to keep his dying wife in this world. "Cook! Go make dinner!"

The wife staggers to her feet, chops onions in the kitchen, fries some rice, says, "It's ready," and brings the wok to the table. Her smile as the husband and their three children hold out their rice bowls is that of the loving mother. In the next instant, beside his wife, after she has fallen to the tatami and died, the husband shouts at the children,

"Keep eating! It's the last meal your mother cooked! Eat while it's hot! Eat!"

The scene captures the ultimate relationship of all living creatures: the parent who stakes her life to preserve the children who have received life from her. With overwhelming wisdom and insight, Juzo Itami portrays this maternal instinct through one meal of fried rice. Though this is a bloodcurdling, ghastly scene, a somehow purified cleanness rises from the screen.

In 1985, the year *Tampopo* was released, society was changing profoundly. The year saw "The International Exposition, Tsukuba, Japan, 1985," passage of the Equal Employment Opportunity Law, the Hanshin Tigers winning baseball's Central

"一億総グルメ" なる言葉が登場。八月十二日、羽田を発って大阪に向かった日航ジャンボ機が群馬県・御巣鷹山の尾根に墜落。真夏に起こった未曾有の航空事故は、私たちの日常は生と死の背中合わせそのものだという現実を容赦なく突きつけ、日本列島は鎮魂の祈りに包まれた。

誰もが、不可視の明日を抱えながら生きている。最期の炒飯を「うまいよ、かあちゃん」と、子らとともに喉の奥に押し込む瞬間は、けっしてスクリーンのなかの一場面でも、ましてやファンタジーでもなかった。

食べなければ生きられない。食べる行為から、誰も逃げられない。食べ止むのはただ一度、死を迎えたときなのだ。そのときが訪れるまで人間がものを食べる姿は、愚直で、けなげで、滑稽で、切なくて、うれしい。

だからこそ映画表現は成立するという確信を最大の原動力として、伊丹十三は『タンポポ』を撮った。

平松洋子（ひらまつ・ようこ）
作家／エッセイスト

東京女子大学卒業後、国内外の食文化と暮らし、文芸と作家を主なテーマに取材、執筆を行っている。２０２２年、『父のビスコ』（小学館）で読売文学賞受賞ほか、著書多数。近著に『ルポ 筋肉と脂肪 アスリートに訊け』（新潮社）。

食べること　生きること

League pennant for the first time in 21 years, the ramen boom, and the coining of a new term "the age of 100 million gourmets." On August 20th, a jumbo jet bound from Tokyo's Haneda airport to Osaka crashed into a ridge on Mt. Osutaka in Gunma Prefecture. Coming at the height of summer, this unprecedented aviation disaster was a blunt reminder of the reality that life and death stand together, and prayers for the repose of souls spanned the Japanese archipelago.

All of us live our lives in possession of an invisible tomorrow. That moment when saying, "This is good, Mom!" along with the children, we push that fried rice deep into our mouths is very much not a fantasy, even if it is only one scene on a screen.

If we do not eat, we cannot live. No one can escape from the act of eating. We stop eating only once, as we face death. Until that moment comes, the figure of a person eating is honest, noble, ridiculous, heartrending, and gratifying. Juzo Itami's very confidence he could express this as a movie was his greatest motivation for making *Tampopo*.

Translation_Ian MacDougall

Yoko Hiramatsu
Author / Essayist

A graduate of Tokyo Women's Christian University, she studies and writes mainly about food, lifestyles, literature and authors in Japan and abroad. Awards she has won include the Yomiuri Prize for Literature in 2020 for *Chichi no bisuko* /"My Father's Biscuits" (Shogakukan). *Rupo kinniku to shibo asuriito ni* / "The Reportage Muscle and Fats Ask the Athletes" (2020) is a recent work.

食べなければ生きられない。食べる行為から、誰も逃げられない。
食べ止むのはただ一度、死を迎えたときなのだ。

（P204『最期の晩餐』平松洋子）

If we do not eat, we cannot live. No one can escape from the act of eating.

We stop eating only once, as we face death.

(P205 "The Last Supper" by Yoko Hiramatsu)

人

生

Life

交響詩『前奏曲』フランツ・リスト

Words of Outsiders

13

Symphonic Poem *Les Préludes* Franz Liszt

「おっぱいの味」

三浦 信

はじめはただ、ラーメンの本を作ろうと思っていた。

本を作る目的には、出版 "者" を名乗る自分にとって作品作りの意味も含まれるわけで、その大義名分は揺るぎないものでなければいけない。編集する素材は自分の人生において必要不可欠な要素であることが絶対条件で、ましてやその完成品は未来に向かって世界の共通言語となり得るものじゃないと。だってこんな便利でモノに溢れてケータイだけでなんでもコトが済む現代に、"わざわざ" 本を作るのだから。それゆえ処女作は自分の最たる興味の矛先として「音」に向かい、稀代の音楽家・三宅純の軌跡を3年かけて追い、彼に関する証言を7カ国48名から集めて紡いだ。

敬愛するボリス・ヴィアンは、ミシェル・ゴンドリーが映画化したことでも知られる名著『うたかたの日々』の序文において、人生で大切なことはふたつだけ。可愛い女の子との恋愛と、デューク・エリントンの音楽と宣言している。そうか、別にひとつじゃなくたっていいんだ。人生におけるもうひとつの必要不可欠な要素・ふたつめの題材を挙げるなら「食」が相応しいと思った。「愛」を選ぶにはもう少し人生の熟成期間が必要だ。そして「食」の日本代表を選ぶなら庶民の自

The Taste of Breast Milk

Makoto Miura

I started out thinking would just do a book on ramen.

My purpose in making a book also includes the meaning of creating a work of art as a "publisher," and I would have to be unwavering in my commitment to this cause. The materials I would edit would absolutely have to be essential elements in my own life, and even more, the completed work would have to be something that could be part of a universal language for the future. After all, in an age so convenient with everything close at hand, where anything can be done with a cell phone, I would be going through the trouble of making a book. Thus for my first attempt, I turned to the most significant focus of my interest, "sound," and tracked the extraordinary musician Jun Miyake for three years, gathering testimony about him from 48 people in seven countries.

Boris Vian, a French writer I greatly admire, declares in the introduction to his novel *Froth on the Daydream* (*L'Écume des jours*, also filmed by Michel Gondry as *Mood Indigo*) that there are only two important things in life: love with a pretty girl, and the music of Duke Ellington. I see. You

分に寿司の選択肢はなく、ラーメンしか
カー同様に海外組も活躍している業界なので。

しかし良いと思われる企画の類は、いつだって真夜
中のラブレター。夜が明けて日の当たる机で読み返せ
ば赤面するほどの恥ずかしさに溢れているのが常。
絞り出したアイデアは薄い出汁のようで、ラーメン
ショップガイドの域を抜け出せず。ましてや街にも世
間にも、単なる情報の類は溢れまくって雑踏に埋も
れている。想像以上の長期に渡るウィズ・コロナの生
活を送る中、頭を冷やし身体を温めるふたつの目的を
兼ねて荻窪の名店、春木屋を訪ねる。昭和の時代から
変わらぬような店内で欲張りな焼豚ワンタン麺が軽快
に、勢いよくどんぶりに盛られていくのを眺めていた
ら、幼い頃に観た『タンポポ』のことをふと思い出した。
そして悶々と頭の中に点在していた点と点が、綺麗に
結ばれたような気がしたのだ。

後日東京のサン＝ジェルマン＝デ＝プレ、はたまた
日本一の古本街である神保町に向かい、幼い頃の記憶
を辿るべく『タンポポ』のパンフレットを手にする。
「私は前から食べ物の映画を作りたかった。食べ物
のイメージというのは、われわれの視覚や聴覚だけで

なく、味覚や触覚まで刺激する、素晴らしい映画的な
素材だと思うのです。食べ物を素材にすれば実に官能
的な映画ができるのではないかと、私は長い間夢見て
きました」（伊丹十三）

監督が映画を作る動機に、単語としてラーメンは含
まれず。あくまでそれが手段であったことが想像され
る。そしてデビュー間もない渡辺謙の証言からも、伊
丹十三のプライオリティがメインストーリーではな
く、サイドストーリーに渡っていたことが確認でき
る。撮影はコチラの方が先だったのだ。

「ほんとはね、一番最初にメインストーリー以外の
エピソードの部分をラッシュで見てね、かなり個性的
な役者さん達の、それぞれ面白いシーンばかりなので、
僕の出るメインストーリーは、やりにくいっていうか、
すごくむずかしいなあ、って思っていたんです」（渡
辺謙）

未来に向けて、世界の共通言語となり得る本を"わ
ざわざ"作る。伊丹十三が西部劇を隠れ蓑にラーメン
映画を作りつつ、食べる行為から生と（性と）死を描
いたように、『タンポポ』そのものを隠れ蓑に、同じ
く「食」を介して未来へのヒントを探る。そんな揺る

don't have to have only one. I decided that "food," another absolutely essential element, would be appropriate as my second subject. To choose "love," I would require a little more time to mature. And as one of the common people, my only choice as the most representative Japanese food was not sushi but ramen. Like soccer, it is a business in which foreign teams are also active.

But a project that might seem like a good idea at some point becomes like a love letter written in the middle of the night. Usually, at dawn, when you re-read it at your desk, you go bright red with embarrassment. The ideas you have racked your brain for are like watery broth and stay below the level of ramen restaurant guides. Even worse, in the city and the world, mere information is overflowing and buried in the hustle and bustle. Pursuing my daily life under the corona pandemic that had gone on far longer than I had imagined, with the dual purposes of cooling my head and warming my body, I visited Harukiya, the famous ramen shop in Tokyo's Ogikubo district. In this restaurant, which has not changed since the 1970s or 80s, watching greedily as fried pork wonton noodles were lightly yet vigorously heaped up in bowls, I remembered *Tampopo*, a movie I had seen as a child. And then

it was as if the separate dots scattered about in my addled brain had come perfectly together.

Some days later, I happened to head to Jinbocho, Tokyo's used-bookstore version of Saint-Germain-des-Prés in Paris, and to refresh my memory, I bought a *Tampopo* movie program.

"I've wanted to make a movie about food for a long time. I think the images of food, stimulating not only sight and hearing but also the senses of taste and touch, will be material for a great film. I have long dreamed about perhaps making a truly arousing movie using food as its subject matter." (Juzo Itami)

The director does not use the word "ramen" in his motive for making this movie. We can imagine that it is only a means to an end. And from the testimony of Ken Watanabe, still fresh from his debut as an actor, we can confirm that Itami prioritized not the main story but the side episodes. These were filmed first.

"As a matter of fact, I first saw rushes of the episodes other than the main story, and they all featured very distinctive actors, and all the scenes were funny and fascinating. So I thought shooting the main story which I was in would be really challenging." (Ken Watanabe)

ざない大義名分がようやく整い、インタビューの準備をはじめ、コラム原稿の発注に取り掛かった。協力者のほとんどが映画『タンポポ』のアウトサイダーであることは問題なかった。むしろその方が「愛」が溢れていくような気がした。

だからこのプロジェクトを終えるに際し、エピローグ代わりに僕個人の思い出を記すことをお許しいただきたい。映画の最後を飾るサイドストーリーが授乳シーンであるゆえ、身勝手ながら自分がノスタルジーに浸ること以外、正しい終わり方を見つけることができなかった。

正直に告白するなら、乳離れのできない子供だった。

正確には小学校2年生まで母の乳房をまさぐっていた。土間があるような秋田の古い実家の2階で畳の上に布団を敷き、夏になれば蚊帳を張って川の字になって眠っていた様子は、『となりのトトロ』でメイとサツキが嬉々としておっぱいをさほど変わらない。ある朝、例の如くおっぱいを探し求めた自分の右手に身に覚えのない感触を得て瞳を開けると、そこは体毛豊かな父の胸板だった、なんてことも。

太平洋戦争では衛生兵だったのに、囲炉裏の前で思わせぶりに日本刀の手入れをしていた祖父は、ちょっと見栄っ張りな頑固者でNHKのニュースを観るためにテレビの前では常に正座をしていた。リモコンはもちろんないし、ボタン式でもない。ガチャガチャと手でチャンネルを回すテレビはもちろんブラウン管。『タンポポ』をはじめて観たのは、そんな古いテレビだったと思う。観た、というよりは目にしたという方が正確かもしれない。奇妙でスケベで、なんだか滑稽なラーメン映画という印象は変わらぬまま、憧れの街東京に根を張ることとなる。

大学は5年通って就職もできぬまま、神保町の出版社でアルバイト暮らし。そこから泣く子も黙る汐留の広告代理店で派遣社員。不向きなスーツを脱ぎ捨てるように2年ほどで逃げ出して、カジュアルなアパレル関係者になりすまして10年ほど勤め上げ、関係者ではない何者かになりたくて個人事業主という肩書きで再び現実からの逃亡生活。そんな新基軸を旗揚げした初年度は、母が天に召された年でもあった。しかも僕の誕生日。不甲斐ない息子を、せめて最後に祝いたい。ガンという名のせっかちな病魔と、そんな想いで闘っていたのかもしれない。

I'm going out of my way to create a book that can become a universal language for the future. While Juzo Itami makes a ramen movie in the guise of a western film, portraying life, (sex), and death through the act of eating, *Tampopo* is, for me, a guise as I search for hints for the future through the medium of food as well. With my cause firmly fixed, I began to prepare for interviews and commissioned manuscripts. It did not matter that most contributors were not involved in the actual movie. On the contrary, it seemed to me that the "love" would overflow that way.

So, upon the conclusion of this project, I ask your forbearance if I put down my own memories in place of an epilogue. Similar to the breast-feeding scene, the side story adorning the movie's end, I was not able to find a good way to end this other than a selfish immersion in nostalgia.

To be perfectly honest, I was a child who would not be weaned.

More precisely, until I was in second grade, I was still seeking my mother's breast. In my family home, an old northern house in Akita with a large earthen floored room, the futons would be spread on the tatami mats upstairs. In the summer we would spread mosquito netting and sleep three nestled against each other, as in the kanji character 川 for "river," in a scene not very different from the happy scenes of Mei and Satsuki in the movie *My Neighbor Totoro*. One morning when, as always, I was seeking my mother's breast, my hand came in contact with something that felt unfamiliar, and I opened my eyes to find my father's hairy chest. As I live and breathe.

My grandfather, a medic during the Pacific War but who would still sit before the sunken hearth and meaningfully polish his *katana* sword, was a somewhat vain and stubborn man who would always kneel in the formal *seiza* position before the TV to watch the NHK news. There was no remote control; neither were there button-type controls. Requiring that you click through the channels by hand-turning a dial, the TV set of course had a cathode-ray tube. When I first saw *Tampopo*, I think it was on an old TV like that. It might be more accurate to say I saw it rather than watched it. My first impression of this strange, lewd, somehow comical movie was unchanged as I grew up and transplanted myself to Tokyo, the city of my dreams.

母は料理が得意な人だった。後にグルマン世界料理本大賞を受賞する栗原はるみを崇拝し、しめ鯖を作る日はやたらとそれが彼女のレシピであることを強調していた。カレーは市販のルーに頼らず、スパイスを自らブレンドしていた。幼心に骨付きチキンカレーの思い出は強烈だ。何故なら血気盛んな父は、どんな経緯かは分からぬも皿に盛られた1杯を母に投げつけたことがあった。怯える母の表情と、時間差でカレーに落とされていた生卵が頬を伝って落ちていく様子は未だに鮮明だ。母亡きあとに、父に反省を促す会話の中で思い出したレシピは以下の通り。

クリスマスのローストチキン。
腹の中に尻から入れたレバーの詰め物。

うずらの卵とソーセージのバーベキュー串。
カレー粉をまぶして。

1日掛かりのスープ作りに驚いた。
1日かけて作るコンソメスープ。

ローストビーフ。

漫画『ミスター味っ子』で知り、リクエストした。
誕生日の9月はメロンをイチゴの代わりに。
誕生日のショートケーキ。

中華煮豚。

なぜかラーメンに使われることがなかった気がする。

麺を冷水で絞めていた記憶。
ミートボール付きミートソーススパゲティ。

お好み焼き。

キャベツはざく切りで、
ソースはマヨネーズと混ぜていた。

海老の水餃子。

僕が学生の頃は冷凍して送ってくれた。

いちごのアイスクリーム。
やさしいピンク色だった。

ほうれん草の海苔巻き。
お弁当の定番。

Still unable to find permanent employment after five years of university, I was getting by working part-time for a publisher in Jinbocho. Then I became a temporary worker at a very intimidating advertising agency in Shiodome. After two years, I fled as if to discard the suit that did not suit me, and then I worked for ten years posing as a casual someone who had something to do with the apparel business. Finally, wanting to be someone more than someone who had something to do with other people's business, I again attempted to escape from reality under the title of "sole proprietor." The first year I launched this new foundation was also the year my mother passed away. On my birthday, of all days. As if she wanted to celebrate a worthless son at the end. She may have fought that evil spirit called cancer with such in mind.

My mother was a good cook. She worshipped Harumi Kurihara, who later won the Gourmand World Cookbook Award, and when she made soused mackerel, she would always emphasize whose recipe it was. She would never use store-bought curry roux, and she blended her own spices. Her unboned chicken curry is a vivid childhood memory. This is because, for some unknown reason, my hot-blooded father once threw a full plate of it at her. The memory of my mother's terrified expression, and the way the raw egg in the curry followed it down her cheek, is still fresh. After she died, the home-cooking recipes I remembered during my conversation with my father urging him to take stock of himself, are as below.

Okonomiyaki:
Shredded cabbage and mayonnaise mixed in with the sauce.

Boiled Shrimp Gyoza Dumplings:
When I was in university, she would freeze them and send them to me.

Strawberry Ice Cream:
A mild pink color.

Christmas Roast Chicken:
Stomach filled with liver paste inserted through the tail end.

Quail Eggs and Skewer-barbecued Sausage:
Covered in curry powder.

One-day Consommé Soup:
I was amazed it took a whole day to make.

焼きおにぎりも忘れがたい。

朝のミニホットドッグとコーヒー牛乳。

もう二度と味わうことのできない味を辿るだけで、目頭が熱くなる。そして残念ながら、母乳で育った自分が、そのおっぱいの味を思い出すことは出来ない。それもまた悲しさに拍車を掛けるのだ。頬を伝って落ちる涙は、しょっぱい。ただこのしょっぱさを、母から授かった生命の味として解釈することは、間違っていないようにも思える。生まれたその日からおっぱいを口にして、僕は今の僕に至っている。その過程で口にしたおふくろの味で、僕の肉体は形成されている。その身体から出た涙の味を形容する言葉が、ひとまず「しょっぱい」としか言いようのないものだとしても、その実態は心地よくて、温かくて、やさしさに包まれているのだ。生命の味は、複雑だ。人生だって、単純じゃない。だから人生は、ドラマになるのだ。

食べることは、生きること。とっても当たり前のことが、とっても深い営みであることを、人生の経年変化を経て理解しはじめている。そしてどんな人生も、ドラマに満ち溢れている。誰だって言いそうなことだけれども、

どんな伝え方をするのかでその奥行きは深くもなれば浅くもなる。そして伊丹十三はとても巧妙にして複雑な手口で時間をかけて、僕らをかなり深いところまで導いたのではないだろうか。随分と引きずり回してくれたけど、言うまでもなくすべてのはじまりはみんなおっぱいなのだ。ずるいぜ、伊丹さん。最後の最後にそんなとっても当たり前で大切で、図らずも見落としてしまいそうなことを、しれっと気づかせてくれるのだから。

母さんへ。
息子は今日も元気にやってます。

三浦 信（みうら・まこと）
出版者

クリエイティブ・プロダクション株式会社コラクソー代表。国内外のアーティスト・クリエイターに焦点を当てたインタビューメディア PORTRAITS.JP を運営。2022 年出版業をスタート。希代の音楽家、三宅純の軌跡を 7 カ国 48 名の証言者から編纂した『MOMENTS / JUN MIYAKE 三宅純と 48 人の証言者たち』が好評発売中。

人生

Roast Beef:

A request of mine after reading the comic "Mr. Ajikko."

Birthday Shortcake:

My birthday is in September, so substitute melon for strawberry.

Boiled Pork, Chinese Style:

Somehow, this was not used in ramen for some reason.

Spaghetti with Meat Sauce & Meatballs:

I remember the noodles were washed in cold water to make them firm.

Spinach Sushi Rolls:

School lunchbox standard.

Also unforgettable are the fried rice balls, morning mini-hotdogs and coffee-flavored milk.

Just toting up the tastes I will never experience again brings tears to my eyes. And sadly, I can't remember the taste of the mother's breast milk on which I was raised. That is another spur to grief. The tears dropping onto my cheeks taste of salt. I feel I am not wrong in interpreting that salty taste as the taste of the life I received from my mother. Putting my mouth to that breast from the day I was born, I became who I am now. My body is formed by the taste of my mother's food I have consumed. Even if there is no better word than "salty" to describe the taste of the tears from this body, the reality is enwrapped in comfort, warmth, and gentleness. Existence has a complex taste. Life, after all, is not straightforward. That is why it can be made into a drama.

Eating is living.

As one age, one comes to understand that such obvious things actually require a very deep level of execution. And every life is full of drama. Anybody can probably express this, but its depth or lack thereof depends on how this is communicated. And surely, over time, in his cleverly complicated way, did Juzo Itami not lead us to a fairly deep place? He may drag us around all over the place, but it goes without saying that the breast milk is the starting point for us all. It's not fair, Mr. Itami. At the very end, you casually brought to our attention something extremely obvious and important, something we were about to overlook.

Dear mother.

Your son is doing well today, as always.

Translation_Ian MacDougall

Makoto Miura
Publisher

Head of the creative production company COLAXO Inc. He runs the website PORTRAITS.JP, an interview media focusing on artists and other creators in Japan and abroad. He began publishing in 2022. Following the extraordinary musician Jun Miyake for three years, he interviewed 48 people in seven countries to compile the book *MOMENTS / JUN MIYAKE — Miyake Jun and 48 Witnesses* which is now on sale.

Juzo Itami
(1933-1997)

 © 伊丹プロダクション

伊丹十三に捧ぐ

TAMPOPO 13

企画・編集・制作：株式会社コラクソー

アートディレクション：高橋 了

寄 稿：菅付雅信、梶野彰一、青野賢一、鍵和田啓介、林 伸次、猫沢エミ、湯山玲子、
長谷部千彩、ヴィヴィアン佐藤、中島敏子、杉山恒太郎、平松洋子、
ウィリー・ブラックモア、ホリー・ジュリエット・ジンバート

撮 影：パーカー・フィッツジェラルド、アヤ・ブラケット、高橋ヨーコ、
コウヘイ・カワシマ、大辻隆広、松本昇大、鈴木陽介、小宮山裕介、伊藤徹也

イラスト：ユウコ・シミズ（表紙）、ピン・ズゥー

インタビュー：サム・ホワイト＆レイニエル・デ・グズマン（RAMEN SHOP, Oakland）、
野村友里（eatrip）、菊池亜希子、田中知之（FPM）、
アイバン・オーキン（IVAN RAMEN, New York）

翻 訳：イアン・マクドゥーガル、トライベクトル株式会社

翻訳協力：鈴木たまみ、野々村万穂、中村明美、加藤寛子

校 閲：菅原海大

Planning, Editing & Production: Colaxo Inc.

Art Direction: Ryo Takahashi

Contributors: Masanobu Sugatsuke, Shoichi Kajino, Kenichi Aono, Keisuke Kagiwada,
Shinji Hayashi, Emi Necozawa, Reiko Yuyama, Chisai Hasebe, Vivian Sato,
Toshiko Nakashima, Kotaro Sugiyama, Yoko Hiramatsu, Willy Blackmore, Holly Juliet Zimbert

Photographs: Parker Fitzgerald, Aya Brackett, Yoko Takahashi, Kohei Kawashima,
Takahiro Otsuji, Shota Matsumoto, Yosuke Suzuki, Yusuke Komiyama, Tetsuya Ito

Illustrations: Yuko Shimizu (cover), Ping Zhu

Interviews: Sam White & Rayneil De Guzman (RAMEN SHOP, CA), Yuri Nomura (eatrip),
Akiko Kikuchi, Tomoyuki Tanaka (FPM), Ivan Orkin (IVAN RAMEN, NY)

Translation: Ian MacDougall, Trivector Co., Ltd.

Translation Assistance: Tamami Suzuki, Maho Nonomura, Akemi Nakamura, Hiroko Kato

Proofreading: Mio Sugawara

発行日：2023 年 7 月 4 日
編集人・発行人：三浦 信
発　行：株式会社コラクソー
印　刷：株式会社八紘美術

©COLAXO Inc.
http://colaxo.jp/

978-4-910808-02-4 C0074

Printed in Japan
無断転載禁止
©All rights reserved